CW00504697

The City of Lo

WHO, WHAT, WHY?

A collection of articles explaining the City of London; its civic traditions, historic offices, people and current purpose.
Plastering over the cracks in your knowledge.

Alderman Alison J Gowman
Master of the Plaisterers' Livery 2019-20

Published by Dowgate Press
382 Shakespeare Tower
Barbican
London
EC2Y 8NJ
Copyright © Dowgate Press 2019

ISBN 978-1-5272-4266-1

Graphic design and typesetting by Bp Media Design

Printed and bound by Initio Design Ltd.

CONTENTS

Mario Testino ©

As an Honorary Liveryman of the Worshipful Company of Plaisterers, I am delighted to introduce this collection of articles which offers Freemen and Liverymen a wider understanding of the role of the City of London today. The articles cover an extensive variety of topics and show how the ceremonial and business aspects of the City can sit happily side by side.

The Livery Companies have been at the heart of the City since mediaeval times, and have made a huge contribution to its pageantry and commercial life. The Worshipful Company of Plaisterers can be immensely proud of the way it has developed over the centuries. It has retained its cherished traditions while adapting to the modern world, making a significant impact through its charitable activities and its support for the craft of plastering with awards and bursaries.

This book offers fascinating glimpses of the work of Livery Companies in the ever-changing City of London: ancient and modern working together.

Camilla

CITY OF
LONDON

The City of London is a complex and fast-moving place. We all need guidance to help us find our way through its intricacies. That is as true for the City's medieval street pattern and the Barbican's highwalk as it is for an understanding of civic tradition, the City of London Corporation and the role of the Livery Companies. Now more than ever, we need to communicate the modern purpose and the great value that these historic institutions bring to the Square Mile and, indeed, the UK.

I therefore welcome the ambition and range of these articles. Written initially to help one Livery Company, the Plaisterers, learn more about civic tradition, the articles are now available to a wider audience. All proceeds are being donated to the Plaisterers' charity of the year, the Museum of London. Written mainly by the current Master Plaisterer, Alderman Alison Gowman, the articles provide a ringside seat and personal view of many of our City institutions.

These first-hand accounts of ceremonies and officials are a great aid in understanding how the panoply of City life comes together. Some of this is little known in the wider community, though these ceremonies and officials are all part of the fascinating historic background to City's contemporary relevance and, indeed, international pre-eminence.

In my role as Lord Mayor, I have the great privilege to participate in - and contribute to - these ceremonies and institutions. There was the Silent Ceremony, for example, when I was sworn in to office; soon after, I made the oath of allegiance before the Judges at the Royal Courts of Justice, one of many high-points of the Lord Mayor's Show. An understanding of these ceremonies helps their modern purpose to become clear.

There is much to read and enjoy in this eclectic and informative volume, so do keep it as a reference for future occasions.

The Right Honourable the Lord Mayor Alderman Peter Estlin

Alderman Alison J Gowman

The City of London: Who, What, Why?

This book is a celebration and description of what I love about the City of London. It is quirky and fusty and steeped in history and tradition whilst at the same time a modern City that punches above its weight on the world stage and is the premier global financial and business centre where people compete to do business, millions rush to visit and many put down long roots to live and thrive.

The publication comes as I start my year as Master of the Plaisterers' Livery Company and my chosen charity is the Museum of London. All of the proceeds of sale of the book will go to the work of the Museum which is an award-winning charity that is right on the doorstep of Plaisterers' Hall and of which I am a Governor. In particular I have singled out the work the Museum does with young people, using a multi-sensory approach and real artefacts from the collection to help students connect with the stories of London and to develop key skills, such as communication and creativity. These are adapted to fit the needs of the students with special educational needs or disabilities, which may include multiple learning disabilities, autism, behavioural difficulties, genetic disorders such as Down's syndrome, speech and language difficulties, sensory impairments, or a combination of several of these. Despite these challenges, students come away from their time not only happy, but having achieved an invaluable experience around historical knowledge and creativity as well as practical understanding and improved communication skills.

It all stems from a decision in 2011 by the Plaisterers' Livery Company who decided that they needed to broaden the understanding of the Livery about the City of London, the Lord Mayor and other elected officers as well as the workings of Guildhall and the physical City surrounding us. In response, I volunteered to write an article a month about the City. Whilst I did write most there are some that I commissioned from Plaisterers and friends and they are acknowledged below with great thanks. Some 80 articles later I was prompted by Plaisterers' Past Master De Bradshaw to put them together into a book for a wider readership. They were reduced to 54 of the best and are largely reproduced here as they were originally written. Thus some seem slightly out of date - chapter 45 on the City and Europe for example - a work in progress as we go to press. Similarly there is no longer the role of Secondary in charge at the Old Bailey - chapter 18. Commemorations of events such as the Great Fire and Waterloo200 might seem time bound but speak of the work of the Corporation in celebrating and marking history in its current context.

As you will see the articles were not written in the order of the book. I have tried to group them around topics starting with the Lord Mayor and the Sheriffs, followed by voting and elections and then the High Officers of the City Corporation. Thereafter I deal with the links with the judiciary which are manifold and lead on to the liaison with the Livery and the freedom of the City. Ceremonial events in the City are set out in chapters 26-33 and then buildings of the City and landmarks followed by the City's role as a local authority and in a wider field across London and the world. Some chapters are difficult to classify simply because the work of the City is so unusual and unique. There are probably many glaring gaps (nothing about the City's work managing 14 open amenity green spaces across Greater London nor about the sterling work of our Environmental Health team and the Port of London Health Authority and very little about the City Police) but as I start as Master Plaisterer I am not intending to write further articles during the year of office. Maybe a second edition in due course.

Those who want to know more will find a wealth of information on the City Corporation's own website www.cityoflondon.gov.uk. I have quoted from two lectures at Gresham College and their website has a depth of lectures and great search-ability www.gresham.ac.uk. A less well known website is that of the Guildhall Historical Association which deals largely with historical events but is worth looking at www.guildhallhistoricalassociation.wordpress.com.

There are many people to thank for their work in the articles and producing the final book. Fellow Plaisterers who have written or contributed to the articles include Past Masters Richard Hanney, Peter Cook and Bill Mahony. Other excellent articles were provided by Barbara Newman CC CBE, Nigel Pullman JP, Annie Allum JP and Jeff Kelly JP. I have also quoted extensively from lectures given by John Clark, Murray Craig and Alderman Sir David Wootton.

Photographs have largely been taken by me or other unnamed friends but I am very grateful to those professional photographers who have kindly allowed me use of their photographs, Mario Testino, Phil McCarthy, Mike Williams and Yvette Woodhouse, as well as the Illustrated London News and the Museum of London.

Finally I am very grateful to Jonathan McCulloch at Bp Media Design for the design and the look and feel of the book, and also to Jonathan Grosvenor for spurring me on when spirits flagged.

Alison Gowman
July 2019

First published June 2019

*I*t is fitting that the first article in this book should be about the Lord Mayor whereas in reality it was the last to be published. The Lord Mayor was a continuous theme and frequently mentioned in so many of the articles that no one exclusive article had been allocated to explain the role.

It seems strange that for the past five years I have penned or arranged (that is borrowed or facilitated) articles about the City of London and omitted to write an article exclusively about the Lord Mayor.

Lord Mayor and Lady Mayoress with the Prime Minister and Philip May at the Lord Mayor's Banquet

Articles have included many speeches and copies of printed interviews by or about the Lord Mayor and his or her role or activities but the extent of the role of the Lord Mayor might still be unclear or misunderstood. Many of the articles have referred to elements of the work of the Lord Mayor but it is only when it is amalgamated that it can be seen what an immense, fulfilling and demanding role it is.

The first recorded Lord Mayor was Henry Fitz-Ailwyn in 1189. The current Lord Mayor is the 691st - thus some have clearly held office for more than the one year that this now the norm. The title 'Lord Mayor' has come about by custom and is not conferred by any charter. In 13th-century documents the Latin term 'dominus maior' is found, and then in English 'Lord Mair' is used in 1414. By the 15th century the prefix 'Right Honourable' was in use. Thus the full title now is 'The Right Honourable the Lord Mayor'.

Some Lord Mayors are household names such as Dick Whittington and William Hardel, who witnessed the Magna Carta. Others have a mixed reputation - such as the Lord Mayor during the Great Fire of 1666 who was unable to appreciate the extent and damage that his inaction was causing in the City. The Magna Carta is of special importance to the City because it is in this document that the right of the City to elect its own Mayor is enshrined and this is the only extant part of the charter still operative and not

Lord Mayor Alderman Peter Estlin speaking at his Lord Mayor's Banquet

revised or subsequently re-enacted. This is not an exclusively male office as there have been two female Lord Mayors to date - Dame Mary Donaldson in 1983 and Dame Fiona Woolf in 2013.

The Lord Mayor now holds office for one year only from the day of the Silent Ceremony in November. The following year is then packed with events such that the Lord Mayor is fully occupied, and ultimately exhausted, by the timetable.

Let me unpack the main constituents of the agenda. First the Lord Mayor is the head of the City of London Corporation. Just to make it very clear his or her remit is the Square Mile of the City of London. He or she works closely with the Mayor of London (the political leader of Greater London). The roles can be confused at first glance and by some overseas visitors; but they are complementary and have a completely different remit. The City Corporation is a uniquely diverse organisation that is more than a local authority. It seeks to support and promote London as a place to live, work, study and be entertained. The Lord Mayor works with other leading members of the City Corporation to make sure that the City's interests are reflected in local and national policy. Such as when in February 2018 the Lord Mayor appeared before the Foreign Affairs Select Committee to discuss what 'Global Britain' meant to the City and the UK professional and financial services sector.

Secondly (in the context of this article written for the Livery) is the role with regard to the Livery, of which the Lord Mayor is the effective head. On the first evening after the Lord Mayor's Banquet, the Lord Mayor and Civic team (the two Sheriffs and Officers) are dined by the Mercers' Livery Company and on the next night he/she is dined by the Grocers. These are immutable dates in the calendar as are many other Livery events through the year. The Lord Mayor seeks to honour many Livery Companies with visits and will present many prizes and awards along the way - indeed the Lord Mayor's attendance at our Plaisterers' Training Awards is a delight and honour to us. Not every company gets a visit from the incumbent Lord Mayor.

The City Ceremonial is closely linked to the Livery - the installation of the Lord Mayor at the Silent Ceremony and the Lord Mayor's Show as well as the church services and other public occasions. These range from the Armed Forces Flag Raising to the switching on of Christmas lights at Leadenhall Market. Additionally the Lord Mayor will host several important dinners each year. As well as the Lord Mayor's Banquet following the installation, the Lord Mayor will host dinners for the Mayor of London and the other London governing bodies in January, the Masters of all the Livery Companies in March, the Ambassadors and Heads of Mission at Easter, the Bankers and Merchants in June, the Judges in July together with dinners for Financial Services and International Trade professionals.

The Lord Mayor has a special link with Government and the Royal Family. Historically, and in constitutional terms, the Lord Mayor is treated rather as the 'premier citizen' (my terminology). In the City of London the Lord Mayor takes precedence over everyone save the Queen. The Lord Mayor is first to be informed of the calling of a general election (after the Monarch) and is first to be informed of the birth of a child of the Sovereign as well as the death of the Monarch. The Lord Mayor is then obliged to announce these matters to the other citizens by way of a public announcement on the steps of the Royal Exchange. The Lord Mayor and Sheriffs attend the Queen at the time of any State visit to meet the visiting Head of State and the City will usually entertain that Head of State at a State Banquet in Guildhall on the second day of the visit at which the Lord Mayor presides.

The Lord Mayor is the international ambassador for the UK's financial and professional services sector. Indeed he or she travels with the seniority of a cabinet minister and thus is accorded a welcome from the local Ambassador who will have been fully involved in creating the Lord Mayor's programme. The remit is to promote this sector in which the UK is the leading exporter of financial services across the world,

At the Silent Ceremony, Lord Mayor Alderman Peter Estlin with late Lord Mayor Alderman Charles Bowman

with a trade surplus of £72bn. London houses more foreign banks, and accounts for more international bank lending, than any other centre. The UK also offers exceptional maritime services, Islamic finance, legal services, insurance, education, and infrastructure financing and delivery. Together, financial and professional services employ over 2.2 million people across the UK, including 1.4 million outside London. There are plenty of good stories to tell and it is the Lord Mayor's job to tell them, at home and abroad. Throughout the year the Lord Mayor is likely to make over 700 speeches and greet tens of thousands of visitors at the Mansion House. At the same time he or she is likely to spend about 100 days abroad and visit some 30 countries in support of the City and the UK.

The Lord Mayor's absences mean that a formal procedure is needed to cope with his or her non-availability. A formal warrant under seal is created to appoint another former Lord Mayor as locum tenens for the duration. There are occasions when the Lord Mayor is not out of the City when a substitute is still needed. This can be dealt with by a Representative Lord Mayor - who is not necessarily a past Lord Mayor. As you can see this can get a bit tricky and technical.

It has become traditional for the Lord Mayor to promote a charity appeal through the Lord Mayor's Appeal. This is in addition to many other charitable endeavours that the Lord Mayor supports. The Lord Mayor promotes the idea of charitable giving with an annual City Giving Day and promotes

Lord Mayor at the Remembrance Day wreath laying

responsible business through the Dragon Awards that have been awarded for over 30 years to businesses and individuals all working to improve the lives and prospects of Londoners. Peter Estlin has chosen the digital agenda to highlight in his year with a theme of Shaping Tomorrow's City Today. He said recently, "Of course, there's only so much I can achieve in a year, but we've launched our digital skills strategy, which is a five-year commitment to driving the digital society forwards. I'm determined that my time as Lord Mayor will not be a pop-up mayoralty but will leave a genuine legacy of social inclusion."

The Lord Mayor's dress is a whole topic on its own as are the insignia of office that are on show at the Silent Ceremony. There is always so much more to explain!

The Lord Mayor resides in the Mansion House during his or her year of office and has a full staff assisting. The senior role is the Executive Director of the Mansion House and Central Criminal Court, a position currently held by Vic Annells. There are three ceremonial officers of the household - the Swordbearer, the Common Cryer and Serjeant-at-Arms (that is one person) and the City Marshal. Although they are seen in formal uniform and splendour on many ceremonial occasions, they double as programme managers who arrange the Lord Mayor's daily programme at home and abroad. In addition the Lord Mayor has diary officers, speech writers and programme managers as well as event planners and administrators. This is not to mention the more personal help with a steward and domestic staff including the caterers and security. All of these work in a great team that ensure that the Lord Mayor and Lady Mayoress are able to perform to the best of their ability during an exciting year of office.

First published June 2018

Members of the Livery will be familiar with the oft-mentioned fact that the Lord Mayor travels out of the City for over 100 days in his or her year of office. Indeed our current Lord Mayor Alderman, Charles Bowman, referred to this at the Banquet on 23rd May at Plaisterers' Hall, saying that to date he has visited 19 countries and will be out of the City for over 106 days.

It is a matter of great importance to the Mayoralty and the City that the Lord Mayor acts as the UK Ambassador for Financial and Professional Services. The Lord Mayor has the confidence of the Government in this role and travels with the status of a Cabinet Minister. The UK is the leading exporter of financial services across the world, with a trade surplus of £72bn. London houses more foreign banks and accounts for more international bank lending than any other centre. The UK also offers exceptional maritime services, Islamic finance, legal services, insurance, education, and infrastructure financing and delivery. There are plenty of good stories to tell and it is the Lord Mayor's job to tell them, at home and abroad.

The Corporation has determined the 20 top overseas markets that it will focus on and the Lord Mayor will expect to visit the top 10 every year and the others on a regular basis. The decisions as to where and when are made in conjunction with the Foreign Office and Department for International Trade. There are strategic reasons for these visits and so there must be alignment and synergy with the visits that other Government ministers and trade envoys are making.

Prior to the visit a lot of the ground work is carried out in conjunction with the local Ambassador and embassy staff. The City's officers are drawn from the Economic Development Office based in Guildhall and the Mansion House but also working closely with The City UK and the various trade bodies and businesses in the City. The Esquires at the Mansion House who are seen in ceremonial guise so frequently are the programme managers who arrange and facilitate the visits - hence the fact that the ceremonial is really only 5% of their and the Lord Mayor's time.

Lord Mayor Alderman Charles Bowman and business delegation in Sao Paolo

Visits are also made to the major UK financial centres and in particular Manchester, Leeds, Birmingham, Edinburgh, Cardiff and Belfast. Many of these cities are key players in the financial services market and employ many workers in the sector outside of London.

You may well wonder what happens on these visits and I can provide some inside knowledge on the recent visit of the Lord Mayor to Brazil as I accompanied him on that visit at the end of April. It is usual for the Lord Mayor to travel with a small business delegation. This might include one of the Sheriffs or other officers of the City or, as in my case, I went as the Deputy Chair of the Green Finance Initiative (a City-led group that promotes Green Finance, with the City as the global market of choice for capital raising and investment). Also in the Brazilian delegation were representatives of the Bank of England, PWC, Columbia Threadneedle and Aberdeen Standard.

Lord Mayor Alderman Peter Estlin in Hong Kong meeting the Financial Secretary Paul Chan

The Lord Mayor's programme is worked out in detail and is crammed full of meetings. On arrival the Lord Mayor is always met by the Ambassador or Consul General - this eases a VIP transit through customs and immigration. It might even lead to a blue light cavalcade through the City to the first appointment - this can depend on the country and the traffic!

The business delegation may have separate events as some meetings for the Lord Mayor may be one to one - especially if it is with a senior or the senior country representative such as the President or Prime

Lord Mayor Alderman Charles Bowman visits JLT in Rio de Janeiro

Lord Mayor Alderman Peter Estlin visiting businesses in Istanbul

Minister.

On my arrival at 6.20am in Sao Paulo after an overnight flight from London, I went into a meeting with the Consul General to brief me on the visit and then another engagement with the Brazilian Banking Association and lunch with the Regional Directors of the Brazilian Development Banks.

At the after-lunch meeting we joined the Lord Mayor who had just arrived from Santiago, Chile where he had been for the previous two days. This was for a meeting with the Brazilian Green Finance Initiative. This group and the London GFI are working together on green finance issues following the signing of a memorandum of understanding by the Chancellor of the Exchequer in Brazil in August last year (I accompanied the Chancellor on that visit). The Lord Mayor spoke about the need to work closely together and the importance of the Brazilian market. He left at the appropriate time to meet a Brazilian Bank for a one to one and I continued a meeting with some more nitty gritty issues to consider.

In the evening we met again at the Consul-General's residence and shared a whisky-tasting and supper with some Brazilian Pension funds.

The next day was taken up by a conference on Green Finance with an audience of 200 people. For me this was preceded by a 45-minute press interview and then a full day of speeches and presentations. The Lord Mayor gave the welcome to the day together with the British Ambassador. While I stayed at the conference for the day, the Lord Mayor went off to visit another three Brazilian banks before returning for the end-of-conference drinks. A light supper followed with the speakers who had been so important in the success of the day.

On the third day we flew off to Rio de Janeiro on an 8.30am flight. Our first stop on arrival was with JLT (see photo) a UK/Hong Kong insurance and reinsurance company who gave a full presentation on their work in Brazil. The Lord Mayor went to lunch with the Rio pension funds and I went to lunch with some oil and gas companies. We met again at an important meeting with the Brazilian National Development Bank who are the main bank funding and driving renewable energy and other projects to combat climate change. Although at the end the Lord Mayor went off for another high level meeting I again stayed to conclude some ideas with the bank.

Our plane back to Sao Paulo got in early enough for us to have an informal supper together to round up our post visit actions. On the fourth day I flew back to London and the Lord Mayor to Lima and, improbably but truthfully, a tryst with Paddington Bear.

The important work is still to be done as the follow-up and briefings are essential to capitalise on the work carried out and the promises and actions agreed. It proved a very successful visit.

3. THE LORD MAYOR'S PATRONAGES AND EXTERNAL ROLES

First published February 2019

The vast majority of events attended by the Lord Mayor start with the host commending the Lord Mayor on his or her busy schedule. That is very true but what is not always clear is exactly what the Lord Mayor does. I want to expound the many patronages and external roles that the Lord Mayor holds for his or her year of office and which equally demand Mayoral time over the course of the year in office.

These roles are exemplified by the Lord Mayor's position as Rector of City University - a role in which

The Silver Mace of City University

he was installed on January 29th this year at the Barbican Centre. The City University was previously the Northampton Institute, in Northampton Square just to the north of the City. City Livery Companies have been involved with the Institute for many years, representing their trades and associations and many are still involved. The Skinners and Saddlers supported the original establishment. Thus it was appropriate for the Lord Mayor to be appointed annually as their Rector in order to continue these links, whereas the University has now extended its studies to match the world-leading financial and professional institutions on its City doorstep. The Lord Mayor is also Vice President of Birkbeck College.

Another close link with the historic Livery foundations is the Lord Mayor's role as an ex officio councillor of the City and Guilds of London Institute. A body that includes other leaders of important bodies; for example, the President of the Royal Academy of Engineering and the Royal Society. Also represented on the Council are 18 Livery Companies who are chosen depending on their respective donations to the Institute.

The Lord Mayor is the patron of the City Livery Club. In this role he or she is invited to the Club's civic lunch or dinner each year. Since 2014 the Lord Mayor has been able to use this event to present the Club's Root and Branch Award to an exemplary Liveryman who has been nominated by a Livery company and chosen by the Club to receive this honour. The Lord Mayor is also the Patron of the Royal Society of St George (City of London branch) whose banquet, on the last evening before Christmas, he or she hosts in the Mansion House. The Lord Mayor is also patron of the Guild of Freemen.

The Lord Mayor is Admiral of the Port of London. It is not surprising to learn that the Lord Mayor has such a close link with the River Thames and the Port as the trading hub for the UK that it once was. The Lord Mayor has a pennant that will fly on any craft in which he or she is carried and on occasion has even steered a boat on the river (see photo). Each year the Admiral of the Port's Challenge is held; this was a race inaugurated by the Lord Mayor and is contested by traditional Thames Waterman's Cutters. In keeping with the concept of traditional rowing, it has fixed seats for up to six rowers and room for a cox and passengers. It is also simply adapted to the role of ceremonial livery barge with extra seating for passengers under a stern canopy. In this form a cutter closely resembles the decorated craft often seen in historical scenes of the Thames in earlier centuries. This event is raced from the Palace of Westminster to Westminster Boating Base, a distance of 1.33 statute miles. The rules require that the cutters are rowed by four oars, must be rigged with their ceremonial canopies and flags, and must carry two passengers. The Lord Mayor as admiral attends but is not required to row.

The Lord Mayor is the Patron of the London Road Safety Council. This organisation brings together elected members and road safety officers from each of the 32 London Boroughs and the City of London. It is unusual for organisations to mix elected members and officers but the ability of these two groups to work together as equal members is useful to share best practice and get things done. The Lord Mayor was helpful in the Council's celebration of its 100 years of work in 2017. The author is the City's representative on the Council and Chair of its Executive Committee.

The Lord Mayor has a close association with many charities for historical and other reasons. He or she is the Vice President of the Court of Governors of Christ's Hospital Foundation. The President is HRH the Duke of Gloucester. The Lord Mayor and Sheriffs attend in state at the annual Speech Day in May at the school. The links go back to the founding of the school, when in 1552 the young King Edward VI responded to an impassioned sermon on the needs of London's poor, and summoned the preacher, the Bishop of London, to talk more about this pressing situation. It was suggested that Edward should write to the Lord Mayor of London to set in motion charitable measures to help the poor.

Lord Mayor Alderman Peter Estlin at Christ's Hospital Speech Day

Christ's Hospital was consequently founded in the old buildings vacated by the Grey Friars in Newgate Street, London, and provided food, clothing, lodging and learning for children without any means. Its sister school with the same historic origins is King Edward's School, Witley, Surrey.

The Lord Mayor's links with the military and Church are several and include as patron of the Reserve Forces' and Cadets' Association for Greater London; vice president ex officio of the Shipwrecked Mariners' Society; co-President of the Friends of St Paul's Cathedral (with the Bishop) and co-President of Heart of the City (with the Governor of the Bank of England).

Some links arise from the actions of previous Lord Mayors. For example the Lord Mayor is the Patron of the Kennedy Memorial Trust due to the fact that the Lord Mayor in 1963 was asked to launch the appeal for funds following President Kennedy's assassination. That was a national appeal for funds for an appropriate memorial to honour the President in the UK. The Fund now provides scholarships and research grants. The Lord Mayor is also an Honorary Trustee of the Treloar Trust, and an annual visit is made by the Lord Mayor with the Masters of all the Livery Companies to see the College in Hampshire. The College was founded in 1907 by then Lord Mayor Lord Treloar.

The links with organisations partly funded or run by the City Corporation might be a more obvious link. The Lord Mayor is Patron of the Guildhall School of Music and Drama and an ex officio member of many of the Corporation's internal committees, most of which he or she will not have time to attend but with whom he or she keeps a close link. Included in these is the City Bridge Trust: the Committee chaired by the author that distributes grants across Greater London.

When I add that the list of such appointments is much longer than summarised here you will see the truth about the Lord Mayor's busy schedule.

Lord Mayor Alderman Sir Andrew Parmley exercising his rights as Admiral of the Port of London

First published March 2012

In writing about the role of the Sheriffs, it is almost inevitable that one starts with the history of this ancient office. After all it dates back to the Middle Ages, is older than any other office in the City of London and pre-dates the institution of the Mayoralty by hundreds of years.

By the time of the Norman Conquest in 1066 the City of London had had for many years two Sheriffs who collected London's taxes on behalf of the royal exchequer and enforced royal justice - an extremely powerful position.

Peter Cook Sheriff 2009-10 Past Master Plaisterer and author of the article

Up until about 1130, the Sheriffs were directly appointed by the King, but when London gained a degree of self-government, it was allowed to choose its own Sheriffs who were approved by the King. By the time an annually elected mayor, who became the chief magistrate of the City of London, was introduced in 1189, the power of the Sheriffs was very much on the wane and they became subordinate to the mayor.

Medieval drawing of Sheriff John Derby in Aldermanic robes c 1445-6. Original drawing held in London Metropolitan Archives.

Then in 1385, the Common Council of London stipulated that the, now designated Lord Mayor of the City of London, should "have previously been Sheriff so that he may be tried as to his governance and bounty before he attains the Estate of Mayoralty".

Much of this situation remained unchanged until the late 19th century, during which period the Sheriffs had large judicial responsibilities attending the Justices at the Central Criminal Court Old Bailey since its original role as the Court of the City and Middlesex. In 1889 the jurisdiction of the Sheriffs was restricted to the City and a new office of High Sheriff of Middlesex created.

So what happens today? Are any of the activities of the past still retained? The answer is that many of the activities of the past are retained today, but most are carried out in a very different manner to that adopted by our forebears.

Take, for example, the prime role of a Sheriff today, which is to support the Lord Mayor in his ambassadorial role of promoting the UK's financial services industry. After the establishment of the office of Lord Mayor the role of the Sheriff has always been subordinate to and supportive of the Lord Mayor and has taken many different forms. Attending to the welfare of Her Majesty's Judges at the Old Bailey continues today, albeit in a different form to that of yesteryear.

Some activities, however, are retained in the same manner as they have been for the past 500 or more years. There continue to be two Sheriffs, it continues to be a pre-requisite for election to the office of Lord Mayor that you have served in the office of Sheriff and the Monarch continues to approve the appointment of her City of London Sheriffs.

Today there are three main aspects to the Sheriff's role:
- *Supporting the Lord Mayor in his or her promotion of the UK financial services industry*
- *Attending to the welfare of Her Majesty's Judges at the Old Bailey*
- *Acting as a link between the Livery, the Mayoralty and the City of London Corporation*

Supporting the Lord Mayor is a multi-faceted activity ranging from, at one end, being an important member of top level delegations meeting with heads of state, Prime Ministers and Ambassadors to encouraging support at home from Ward Clubs and scout groups, at the other. Constantly on public display, recognising that the role you play is important to many different people who are observing your every move, monitoring your performance as it influences their enthusiasm and commitment to supporting the role of Lord Mayor.

Looking after the welfare of Her Majesty's Judges at the Old Bailey involves providing about 500 interesting guests for lunch over the year of one's term of office. This activity has a twofold benefit, one to the judges and the other in the communication of the workings of the Central Criminal Court to the guests and the wider public. Guests experience not only the expertise and intellect of the judges but also their remarkable humanity. The judges for their part are able to relax for an hour, away from their complex cases - mainly murders - while hearing a variety of views and opinions and learning about a multitude of different walks of life described to them by their guests.

The past 10 years have seen an increase in the activities of the Sheriffs in widening the activities of the Mayoral Team. There have been occasions when all three members have been performing at different functions at the same time. This approach can, with careful control, be further exploited to the benefit of the Mayoralty.

Although the basic roles of the two Sheriffs are similar, there are differences in emphasis. This is right and proper in order to assist the Aldermanic Sheriff in his or her activities of preparing to become Lord Mayor in the future. This requirement needs to be incorporated in the job descriptions of the two Sheriffs.

The Non-Aldermanic Sheriff is often referred to as the 'Livery Sheriff' in that any member of the Livery is entitled to stand for this office. It also illustrates the importance of the Sheriff's role as a conduit between the Livery, the Mayoralty and the City of London Corporation. The interrelationship between these three entities is complex and, like the shrievalty, has changed over the centuries.

If the undoubted wealth of talent contained within these three entities is to be fully harnessed to the benefit of the City of London as a whole, there is a requirement to examine the willingness of all three parties to determine how better to utilise this potential.

Charter granted in 1199 by King John confirming the right of the citizens of London to elect the Sheriffs - original held in the London Metropolitan Archives

Past Master Peter Cook
Sheriff of the City of London 2009-10

First published April 2018

W e are very grateful to Sheriff Neil Redcliffe, who has taken time out of his very busy schedule to write this month's article. Enjoy this fascinating insight!

As many of you know, each Midsummer's Day at the Guildhall the Livery elects two Sheriffs, who are admitted to office on 28th September and the office lasts for just one year. The Aldermanic Sheriff aims to use his term as Sheriff to prepare for the higher office of Lord Mayor, while the Lay Sheriff, sadly now referred to as the Non-Aldermanic Sheriff, has a responsibility to liaise with the Livery, to advise them on the activities of the Mayoralty and update them on key areas of progress.

The office of Sheriff is an ancient one; its roots lie in Anglo Saxon England, when the 'Shire Reeves'

Alderman and Sheriff Vincent Keaveny's badge of office as Sheriff

were tax collectors for the monarch. In medieval times the Sheriffs, along with the Lord Mayor and Aldermen of the City of London, were the judiciary officiating at periodic Sessions at Newgate Prison. Later, a formal Court House - the Old Bailey - was added. Today the primary role of the Sheriffs is to support the Lord Mayor, who is the principal ambassador and key spokesman for the City of London Corporation and the Business City. The Lord Mayor's primary responsibility is to promote the City and the UK's financial and professional service industries at home and abroad. Our current Lord Mayor, Alderman Charles Bowman, will travel extensively - to 29 countries for almost 100 days of his one-year term of office - tirelessly flying the flag for Britain as a place in which to do business and promoting British businesses overseas.

The Sheriffs play a key role at home and abroad, not only by accompanying the Lord Mayor, but also by carrying out specific 'deputising' activities. I have recently returned from a 14-day Mayoral trip to Australia and New Zealand; while in March my fellow Sheriff, Alderman Tim Hailes, accompanied the Lord Mayor to China and Hong Kong.

The Sheriffs are also responsible for supporting the Lord Mayor's extensive charitable works. The Lord Mayor, together with his two next likely successors (subject to election of course) - Alderman Peter Estlin and Alderman William Russell - have established a three-year programme of charitable works, with the ambitious objective of touching the lives of one million people. The three charities supported each tackle a key area of need: adult mental health, mental health in children and the issues of youths who have nowhere to go and nothing to do. The charities - the Samaritans, Place to Be and Onside Youth Zone - will benefit from having longer term support and hence a much more efficient administrative structure. As part of our support we will be holding a spectacular fundraising 'Sheriffs in Wonderland' Ball at Guildhall on September 21st.

The Sheriffs also play an important role at the Old Bailey, where we reside during our year in office. Our role is described as 'officiating at the sessions at the Central Criminal Court,' but I think of it as looking after the well-being of Her Majesty's Judges by entertaining them to lunch and making sure that the Central Criminal Court is fit for purpose. The former is an important ambassadorial role the Sheriffs undertake on behalf of the City of London Corporation, and we invite guests from all walks of life - be it business, politics, education, religion, the arts and culture - promoting the business and social objectives of the City Corporation, and also serving to remind attendees that we have the best judiciary and legal system in the world.

In addition to supporting the Lord Mayor and the Judiciary, we Sheriffs also have important charitable objectives in our own right; we promote and help to raise money for the Old Bailey charity, the Sheriffs' and Recorder's Fund. Living at the Old Bailey I witness some of the most shocking cases our country has to face. We observe cases involving murder, terrorism and rape, and daily I hear stories that fill me with

Lord Mayor Alderman Charles Bowman starts the Magical Taxi Tour 2018 in the presence of the Alderman and Sheriff Tim Hailes and Sheriff Neil Redcliffe

Sheriff Neil Redcliffe attending the Glovers' Banquet

horror. Society tends to shun people who have been in prison and, after often extremely long sentences, many prisoners are released with nowhere to go, nothing to do and no one who cares about them. It's no wonder that there is a big percentage of prisoners who almost immediately re-offend. For over 200 years the Fund has been helping ex-offenders make a new start in life and has endeavoured to relieve the hardship for the families of serving offenders by contributing to the basic support systems which underpin most people's lives: a decent education, a job, a stable family and a home.

As mentioned earlier, the Lay Sheriff has a responsibility to liaise with the Livery, which is facing interesting challenges. Many believe that the movement is facing an existential threat, similar to what happened in the late 1800s when a Royal Commission looked at whether the Livery movement had a social purpose. The Pan Livery Project co-ordinated by the Mercers' Company, and so far involving 77 Livery Companies, has recommended that the Livery brings together its external philanthropic initiatives, such as Heritage Crafts & Modern Skills, Employability for the Young, Helping Prisoners become 'job ready' etc, under a single umbrella heading on the theme of 'Employability' with a launch date in the current Mayoral Year.

As well as its many responsibilities, the Sheriff's year is packed with business and non-business events. But for me, two highlights of my year so far have been the Sheriffs' Bravery Awards and the Magical Taxi Tour. British Transport Police Constable Wayne Marques was first on the scene at the London Bridge Terrorist attack in June 2017, when he single-handedly took on three knife-wielding terrorists. PC Marques was mercilessly stabbed by the terrorists, who came very close to killing him, and only the huge efforts of his colleagues, who arrived at the scene soon after, ensured that he survived. It was my privilege to present PC Marques with the City of London's Sheriffs' Award in October and I found him to be a charming and humble young man who was delighted to be recognised for his efforts.

The Magical Taxi Tour is organised by Phil Davis and the Hackney Carriage Drivers' Livery Company. After a shockingly early alarm call the whole Civic Team, the Lord Mayor and Lady Mayoress, both Sheriffs and their Consorts dressed in full ceremonial - scarlet gowns, badges etc. - gathered at Canary Wharf for breakfast with around 150 seriously ill children. The children, many of them terminally ill, along with a sibling or friend and parent or minder are driven to Paris by taxi to spend the weekend at EuroDisney. Just meeting these children and seeing their excitement at breakfast, having photos taken with them, meeting their parents and hearing their stories was humbling and uplifting.

Unbelievably, my wife, Emma, and I are already six months into our term and, although it has shot past in a flash, we are both loving every moment. The 2018 Shrieval election is less than three months away and it is likely to be hotly contested. I urge all Liverymen to find out who the candidates are and think carefully who to choose when they attend Common Hall on 25th June.

Neil Redcliffe
Sheriff of the City of London 2017 - 2018

First published June 2017

What every loyal Liveryman should do on Midsummer Day.

By time-honoured tradition the Livery are summoned on every Midsummer Day to Great Hall, Guildhall, to meet as the Livery combined to elect, among other officers, the two Sheriffs of the City of London. This is to meet in Common Hall. This is a term used to describe a gathering of liverymen, and often associated with an election. Common Hall is also held by the Plaisterers in July and it is just as important to attend then!

Common Hall in Guildhall is an event with which Plaisterers are familiar as they attended this event in 2009 to elect Past Master Peter Cook as Sheriff for that year.

Newly elected Sheriffs Aldermen William Russell and Peter Estlin with Lord Mayor Alderman the Lord Mountevans June 2016

The formal calling to meet and ceremony are of great historic importance. The office of Sheriff is older than any other in the City of London (including the Lord Mayor) and dates back to the Anglo Saxon period of the seventh century. The right to choose their own sheriffs was granted to the citizens of the City in 1199 by Charter. Elsewhere in the country the Sheriffs are chosen (in fact 'pricked' out of a list of names) by the Queen. Since 1585 Sheriffs have been elected on Midsummer Day and they take office on the vigil of St Michael the Archangel (28th September). Having this ancient right it is beholden upon the Livery to exercise it fully and faithfully. "Hereof you are not to fail."

This is a very popular event and if you want to attend it is best to get a ticket in advance via the Clerk. Last-minute attendees can be allowed in but it takes longer for your name to be checked off on the list. Indeed the Great Hall begins to fill from much earlier in the day as many liverymen seek a preferred seat.

It is accepted that this is a three-line whip for all Masters. As will be imagined, Masters will wear gowns and badges but usually over normal business day dress. Some traditional Liverymen might wear morning coats but otherwise business attire with the occasional hat (ladies) and gloves (all). The Masters sit in the first few rows of the Great Hall and make for a very colourful and intimidating audience. The Liverymen sit behind with an overflow in the Old Library linked up with live audio visual links. There are about 30,000 Liverymen at the last count and so not all can expect a seat or even a place. On average about 1,500 attend.

The formal ceremony begins with a procession of the Masters led by the Livery Committee. The Masters process in order of precedence, juniors first. The Livery Committee and the Masters of the Great Twelve Livery Companies process beyond the body of the Hall to sit on the dais facing the Livery arrayed before them. Just before noon the procession of the Lord Mayor commences. The Aldermen will have been waiting in their Court Room in readiness for the nod. The procession includes the Sheriffs' Chaplains, the Secondary and Under Sheriff (in charge of the Old Bailey), the Remembrancer, Comptroller and City Solicitor, Common Serjeant, Chamberlain, Town Clerk, Sheriffs, Aldermen below the Chair, Recorder, Aldermen above the Chair, City Marshal, Chaplain to the Lord Mayor, the Mace and Sword (people carrying the same) and the Lord Mayor. As they enter the Great Hall everyone stands in silence in respect to the Lord Mayor.

The Aldermen are accompanied by their Beadles who carry the mace relating to their Ward, which is the symbol of the authority of the Alderman. Those in the procession all carry posies and the floor of the dais (the Hustings) is scattered with sweet smelling herbs. Everyone on the dais has a designated seat.

Once everyone is seated, the Common Cryer and Serjeant-at-Arms (who carries the Mace) proclaims silence and directs "all persons to be uncovered in the Hall" and "all those who are not liverymen depart this Hall on pain of imprisonment". This is followed by the opening of the Common Hall with an "Oyez, Oyez, Oyez".

The Recorder has the first role to inform the Livery of the purpose of the meeting being: to elect the Sheriffs. The Lord Mayor and Aldermen who have served in the office of Sheriff then leave the Hall and wait in the Print Room where they can watch proceedings on a digital screen.

The Common Serjeant and the two Sheriffs come forward to the front of the dais and the names of each candidate in nomination for Sheriff for the coming year will then be announced by the Common Serjeant. If there are only two names then they are duly elected. However, if there are more than two there is a show of hands in the Hall, a serious count of the voters and the possibility of an adjourned election.

Each of the newly elected prospective Sheriffs come forward to declare their consent to act as Sheriff and make a short speech thanking the Livery.

There are also elections for the roles of Bridgemasters, Aleconners and Auditors.

After the elections and ceremonial are complete, the Common Cryer declares an end to proceedings and declares God Save the Queen, to which all assembled respond with a hearty rendition.

Monday, 24th June 2019

Election of Sheriffs for the City of London

Candidature of Alderman Professor Michael Mainelli

To the Liverymen of the City of London

My Lords, Ladies and Gentlemen,

My colleagues on the Court of Aldermen support my nomination as a candidate for the ancient office of Sheriff of the City London for 2019/20. Therefore, with a sense of honour and enthusiasm, I offer myself to the Livery at the election to be held at **Common Hall in Guildhall on Monday 24th June 2019 at 12 noon**. If a poll is demanded, may I ask for your further support by voting in my favour at a ballot on **Monday 8th July 2019**, also at **Guildhall**.

I was born in the USA, and educated at Harvard University, Trinity College Dublin, and the London School of Economics where I was also a Visiting Professor. I began my career in scientific research in aerospace and cartography in the USA and Switzerland, creating the first digital maps of the world.

I entered the City of London in 1984 ahead of Big Bang, becoming a partner in 1987 with BDO Binder Hamlyn, and in 1995 a Director of Ministry of Defence research. During a mergers & acquisitions spell in merchant banking with Deutsche Morgan Grenfell, I co-founded Z/Yen, the City of London's leading think-tank, promoting societal advance through better finance and technology. We are perhaps best known for the Global Financial Centres Index, Global Green Finance Index, and Long Finance.

I am proud to serve as Alderman for Broad Street since 2013; President of Broad Street Ward Club; Trustee of the Lord Mayor's Appeal, Lord Mayor's Show, Lord Mayor's 800th Anniversary Awards Trust, Christ's Hospital, and Morden College; non-executive director of the United Kingdom Accreditation Service; Emeritus Professor of Gresham College and Fellow of Goodenough College; and Council Member for City & Guilds.

I am a passionate supporter of the Livery as Immediate Past Master of the World Traders, Honorary Liveryman of the Worshipful Companies of Furniture Makers, Water Conservators, and Marketors, Craft-Owning Freeman of the Watermen & Lightermen, and member of the City Livery Club and Guild of Freemen.

My wife, Elisabeth, is from Bavaria. Elisabeth trained in hotel management and has worked in Germany and London, where she became a personal assistant to the managing partner of a large accountancy firm. We married in 1996 and have three children. She continues to work at her events company, and is a director of a property management company. Elisabeth is a Liveryman of the Worshipful Company of Masons and a Freeman *Honoris Causa* of the World Traders.

My interests include skiing, woodcarving, dicing with bagpipes, racing sailboats, and dabbling in German, Italian, and French, but even worse Mandarin. As former Thames barge owners restoring S B Lady Daphne, we retain deep links with the sailing barge community and the venerable Thames Match (1863).

Change is a City constant. I want to work to continue to keep the City pre-eminent as the world's leading professional, business, legal, technical, and financial services centre, championing the three C's of Commerce, Community, and Charity. If elected I will do my utmost to uphold the noble traditions of the Shrieval office. It would be a privilege to use my experience to support the Lord Mayor's and City of London Corporation's programmes promoting the City and the UK in all their aspects.

I have the honour to be, my Lords, Ladies and Gentlemen, your obedient servant,

Professor Michael Mainelli FCCA FCSI (Hon) FBCS CITP FIC CMC MEI
Alderman and World Trader - www.mainelli.org

Address for Shrieval candidate Alderman Michael Mainelli 2019

The procession is formed in reverse order and those on the dais leave Great Hall, again in silence save for the clatter of spurs and heels. The Livery can feel pleased at the result of the proceedings and most return to the various Halls to enjoy a celebratory lunch.

Newly installed Sheriffs Alderman Vincent Keaveny and Liz Green with spouses Amanda and Peter; September 2018

7. A CONTESTED ELECTION AND WHAT HAPPENS NEXT

First published September 2018

Avid readers will recall the procedures at the Midsummer Common Hall when all Liverymen are invited to attend and elect two Sheriffs. There was a hot contest for these roles in 2018, which prompts this further and more detailed explanation.

The Court of Aldermen had approved Alderman Vincent Keaveny to be the Aldermanic Sheriff (a process that takes time and thought). The three other Liverymen were nominated by fellow Liverymen to be considered for the role of Sheriff. With four candidates for two places it is fair to say that the hustings and general noise about the election was quite loud. The local free City newspaper, City Matters,

Voting for the successful candidate Liz Green June 2018

ran several articles on the candidates; each candidate held meetings for their supporters and all were seen at many lunches, dinners and events around the City. Each wrote a full and compelling manifesto with their reasons to stand and be elected. The three non-Aldermanic candidates all declared that Vincent should receive the elector's other vote.

Common Hall does not allow proxy or postal voting - everyone had to turn up. Thus on June 25th (the nearest working day to June 24th) the Great Hall of Guildhall was full as were the overspill rooms of the Livery Hall and the Old Library.

Shortly after the preliminary formal opening of the Common Hall it is a convention that the Aldermen who have already served as Sheriff leave the dais with the Recorder. The purpose is that they do not seek to interfere with the election about to take place. They retire to the Print Room where they view the event on a close circuit TV screen.

The proceedings are then overseen by the Common Serjeant who is the second senior judge at the Old Bailey together with the two serving Sheriffs. The names of each candidate are announced by the Common Serjeant. They are called in turn to make a speech of no more than four minutes and then the vote is put to the assembled Liverymen and women. This is traditionally given by a show of hands. However, if anyone considers that the poll was not clear or the count not right then they can demand a formal second poll. This means that the Common Hall will be adjourned to a date 14 days later for the further poll to be held. At that time anyone wishing to vote needs to attend in person and complete a voting slip, which is counted and determined on that date. No votes are carried over; everyone needs to turn up again. However, as timing is quite tight for the candidates to then prepare for office in September, there is every incentive to determine the outcome on Midsummer Day.

Successful Sheriffs 2018 Liz Green and Alderman Vincent Keaveny

In order to help the clarity of the voting there was an innovation this year, to give every attendee four coloured pieces of paper, each one representing a candidate. Keaveny - white; Fleck - pink; Green - yellow and Rhys - orange. Thus when these were held aloft the myriad officials could more easily see the vote and the count would be more accurate.

Of course, with the electorate in three rooms this made it less clear to the audience as only the Sheriffs and Common Serjeant could see the screens to the subsidiary rooms.

However the count came out very decisively, Keaveny 1,174; Green 748; Fleck 387 and Rhys 122.

A moment's hiatus ensued as the Hall waited to see if anyone wanted to demand a poll but thankfully they did not. The two winning candidates were then required to make a further speech in which it is critical that they state that they are willing to take up office and consent to act as Sheriff - as well as thanking the Livery for the election.

Common Hall in Great Hall, full with Liverymen waiting to vote

After the election and ceremonial are complete, the Common Cryer declares God Save the Queen, to which all assembled respond, God Save the Queen. Certainly this year with more than usual acclaim that no one would need to return to vote again and that the process could now speed along to the next stages.

The two candidates spent the next couple of hours visiting as many Liverymen dining in the various halls as they could. The Plaisterers were dining at Tallow Chandlers Hall where the losing Richard Fleck is a liverymen and was present. A brave face was put on by all as the winners arrived and were clapped in and congratulated.

The Sheriffs elect (as they now are) start a busy time preparing for their year. They must form a Shrieval Chain Committee who help them fund the cost of each Sheriff's chain and brooch for the consort; they will be preparing to host their supporters who contribute to the Chain at a lunchtime drinks reception and chain presentation ceremony in mid-September; they will be preparing the admission ceremony that takes place on September 28th and then working with the Lord Mayor to create the Lord Mayor's banquet. Meanwhile the Sheriffs also prepare a business plan for the year; ensure that they have the right clothes and other ceremonial garb and arrange their affairs to spend a full year at the Old Bailey.

The Admission ceremony is held at noon in the Great Hall on September 28th (in essence the day before the next Common Hall when the next Lord Mayor is elected). While it is a ceremony that any Liveryman can attend it is usually only attended by the invited guests of the two Sheriffs (some 250-300 people). The Lord Mayor presides with all the Aldermen and the Liverymen of the companies of the Sheriffs who have to make two oaths to the Queen to faithfully fulfil the office of Sheriff. It is declared in unison by both Sheriffs - something I often feel that they should practise with a bit more care beforehand!

The outgoing Sheriffs are disrobed and their chains removed and they in turn help their successors to be gowned and wear their own chains for the first time. This is a very moving ceremony carried out with decorum and solemnity. At its conclusion the invited guests all assemble to share the Sheriffs' breakfast - of course eaten at lunch time. The invite suggests that this will not usually end before 3.30pm. There are speeches and much enjoyment as the new Sheriffs polish up those chains to start a year of commitment and service. Meanwhile, back at the Old Bailey the rooms of the departing Sheriffs have been thoroughly cleaned and new signs put up on the doors announcing the new Sheriffs in residence. The start of another amazing year.

First published April 2012

For many people the existence and role of an Alderman seems a bit unclear and obscure but probably sounds important and interesting. Many Liverymen are embarrassed to ask as they feel that they should know. This article aims to do some explaining but, as space is limited, I will touch on the generalities and hope that I will be able to explain more at another time or in person.

First it is important to know that the City of London is the only local authority that elects Aldermen. We are part of the City's governance under the Court of Common Council - that is the name for the Corporation of London's governing body. Already you will see how different the City is! As local government members Aldermen are subject to the Representation of the People Act and other local government legislation. We are elected for a six-year period and can be re-elected until we reach the age of 70. Each of the 25 wards in the City has one Alderman. Plaisterers are in Aldersgate Ward and the Alderman of Aldersgate is Nick Anstee - Liveryman and Past Lord Mayor. My ward is Dowgate, which has as its main feature Cannon Street station and four Livery Halls.

The Court of Aldermen

The City's Common Council and Aldermen are not party political and so when we stand for election we need to be able to convince the electorate that we will do a good job for the ward based upon our ideas and experience. Once elected we are all unpaid. We have a major role to perform in ensuring that our electors (residents and business voters) know that they can raise issues and receive assistance from their elected representatives. I keep in touch with mine and have a website with monthly updates about the issues of the day. Concerns that come up most regularly are the issues of disruptive and noisy road works.

The Aldermen sit on the usual committees as in any local authority - finance, planning, community services etc. The Common Council meets each month and is open to the public - we welcome the public, so do come along and see what we do. I sit on the City of London Police Committee, Standards Committee, City Bridge Trust and City of London Freeman's School as well as chairing the Energy and Sustainability Sub Committee. It should be remembered that the City's role extends far outside the Square Mile as we look after many open spaces such as Hampstead Heath and Epping Forest, run the three major wholesale markets (of which two are outside the City at Billingsgate and Spitalfields) and are the Port of London Health Authority that runs the Heathrow Quarantine Centre.

The Aldermen sit in a separate court as well: the Court of Aldermen. We have a separate meeting room, the 1960s extension in Guildhall Yard. Our business is mainly carried out in the two committees to which we all belong and relates to matters such as the budget for the Lord Mayor and the Mansion House, issues of protocol and the progression and approval of Aldermanic candidates to the shrievalty and mayoralty. The Aldermen also regulate the Livery Companies and determine whether new organisations can become livery companies and ensure that they have passed the requirements of funding and membership. Existing companies need approval of the Aldermen if they want to change ordinances, add numbers or make other significant changes in their regulations. We also approve applications for the freedom of the City that are linked to Livery company membership.

The Aldermen are on the track to be considered for future Sheriff and Lord Mayor. That additional role and privilege leads them to be involved in many other areas of the work of the City. They are part of the host team at all the major City banquets - the banquets for the Livery Masters (held each year in March at the Mansion House), similarly for the Ambassadors, Bishops, Judges as well as for the Chancellor of the Exchequer and to honour City businesses and the Lord Mayor's Dragon awards (for corporate responsibility). Other smaller events occur, for example, when the President of Colombia visited the Lord Mayor in November a small lunch party included me together with other Aldermen and business people who have a connection with that country. The Lord Mayor's busy programme involves many inward visits and initiatives that the Aldermen, according to their expertise and interest, might be

Aldermanic Gowns ready to be worn

photo: Mike Williams

Aldermen taking part in the Lord Mayor's Show

involved in. For example, I attended the Lord Mayor's breakfast meeting for City businesses with The Rt Hon Caroline Spelman MP to discuss the Government's intentions in respect of Rio+20 (the UN Conference on Sustainable Development) where my role on sustainability played its part.

What most of the Livery see on a regular basis is our ceremonial support of the Lord Mayor and Livery at many events. Common Hall in June and September is when the formal elections of the Sheriffs and Lord Mayor take place. We parade in with our Beadles and sit with the Lord Mayor viewing the proceedings. There are many other events such as the recent United Guilds Service in St Paul's where together we represent the City in a formal way. The most exciting event of the year is the Lord Mayor's Show in November. The Aldermen ride in carriages before the Lord Mayor's coach and enjoy interacting with the crowd along the route. Halfway through the parade the Lord Mayor stops at the Royal Courts of Justice and we are all summoned to the Lord Chief Justice's Court for the formal swearing in of the Lord Mayor before the Judges who are fully robed together with a small black tricorn hat on top of their full bottomed wigs - pure spectacle! This is not to mention the Remembrance Sunday service at St Paul's and the subsequent military remembrance and parade at the Royal Exchange when black top hats are the order of the day.

By way of summary the role throws one into the most interesting and (on the first occasion) quite terrifying situations but it is never boring. I have not recorded the fact that the Aldermen are all JPs in the City of London (a pre-qualification to be an Alderman), nor the necessity of being involved in and part of the Livery and knowing your ward, its Ward Club and the people who are your voters. Finally, why is there a photo of me with Colin Firth? I recently hosted the lunch following the grant of his freedom of the City. A definite perk of the job.

*Colin Firth receives the freedom of the City flanked by Alderman Sir Roger Gifford, Richard Regan CC
the author and Chamberlain Chris Bilsland*

First published March 2013

Liverymen will be aware that they are entitled to vote at Common Hall each year for the selection of the Sheriffs and the Lord Mayor. However, March 20th and 21st, 2013, heralds the election for the City of London Corporation as a local authority. Like many of the City traditions, this election is out of sequence with all other local authorities and is significantly different because voters consist not only of the individual 9,000 (approximately) residents but include people who are either running their own businesses or who are nominated by their businesses to vote.

The election is for the 100 Common Councilmen who represent the 25 wards in the City. (The election for the 25 Aldermen takes place every six years and is timed by reference to the individual Ward and that Alderman's date of election.)

Plaisterers' Hall stands in Aldersgate Ward. This is a predominantly residential ward comprising the western part of the Barbican Estate. There are five members but as the relative numbers of voters between the separate wards has changed Aldersgate will increase its member representation by one this year. This increase in members now matches the number as described in John Stow's description of London in 1589 - thus the cycle of City life turns.

Vote2013 logo

Professor Tony Travers of the London School of Economics (a pre-eminent expert and academic on the topic of London governance) lectured at Gresham College in January 2013, about the governance and voting system of the City of London. His lecture set the system in a historical context and is worth reading or watching on www.gresham.ac.uk. He draws out, in particular, the fact that the City's governance ensures that, while the rest of the UK has rather a patchy and undeveloped local government system, the City has always been organised to provide the metropolis with an infrastructure that allowed it to grow and prosper.

By the early part of the 19th century the City of London was resisting pressure for local government to be provided throughout the capital. This led the City to appear increasingly unique and unreformed. This view is still held by some today. The 21st-century system of elections, governance and terminology is one that would have been recognisable in 1832. The independence that has been maintained through the centuries now looks unusual and, arguably, outmoded.

List of voters in Dowgate Ward

Professor Travers suggests that although it can be argued that the City of London is less democratic than other Councils it is clearly more democratic than the huge number of quangos that run public services in Britain today. Prof Travers concludes: "The City of London has proved adept at evolving to survive for about 1,000 years. It would be surprising if it did not outlast many, and possibly most, of today's political institutions."

So how could you participate in the vote? It is clear that all residents within the City have a vote in the usual way. The business vote is the unusual element of the City elections. If you are a sole trader and run your own business in the City then you would be entitled to a vote. Similarly a partnership (typically old style solicitors' and accountants' firms) will have a vote for each equity partner since they are, in fact, the people who are liable to pay the rates. (Until 1969 a business vote of this kind existed in all local authorities). But as most businesses in the Square Mile were now established as corporate bodies (in a legal sense), the business vote was becoming less representative of the businesses and workers in the City. Thus in 2005 the franchise was extended to all businesses (including Livery Companies). Votes are allocated to the qualifying body depending on the number in the workforce. For example, up to nine workers gives an entitlement to one vote but up to 100 employees gives an entitlement to 11 votes. The corporate body concerned completes the form with the names of the individual voters who then become voters direct on the register and act in their own capacity without any need to represent the views of their employer. The individual voters will receive information direct to them and will attend the Polling Station in an individual capacity to vote secretly. Postal and proxy voting is allowed but online voting has not yet arrived in the City.

You might wonder why I have given two dates for the election. Traditionally in the City the election is called the Wardmote. This is a call to the electorate to attend at a meeting chaired by the Alderman who is the legal returning officer and including the Ward Beadle who acts as the Master of Ceremonies. On the first date the Wardmote is formally opened and the candidates are given a chance to address the electorate gathered (usually not into double digits in most wards). The next day is the voting at the polling station between 8am and 8pm and concludes with the Wardmote being reconvened to announce the result. Although the language has been modernised over the years, the Beadle traditionally commences the Wardmote with the words:

"Oyez oyez oyez all manner of persons who have anything to do with this Court of Wardmote for the ward of … holden here this day before the Worshipful Alderman … draw near and give your attendance. God save the Queen."

As you can imagine with the Alderman in his/her violet gown trimmed with bear fur and the Beadle in caped robe and carrying the Ward mace, it has traditional and occasional farcical moments. Strictly speaking, if there is a tie in the voting then the Aldermen can choose the winner. Time-honoured tradition shows that this is best done by way of drawing straws although, on one occasion, the Aldermen decided to have a new election and sadly in the interim one of the candidates died.

The elections in March are likely to be hotly contested. Although they remain non-party political there is always the possibility of individuals standing under a party banner. This is despite the fact that the major political parties have all declared that they do not wish to see the City of London elections politicised - there is some measure of general support from Government and Westminster to the City model.

In order to stand as a Common Councilman there are certain qualifications. Despite the usual ones of being over 18 and a citizen of the EU, the individual must be registered on the City Ward Lists and be a Freeman of the City. The qualification as a Freeman of the City is not one that would be used to debar anyone and a fast track process will be put in place if necessary. The need to be on the Ward List is important and ensures the close connection between the candidates and the City. Some Livery Companies have allowed their Liverymen who are interested in standing for election to be on the electoral roll for the livery hall and this, in turn, ensures a close link between the City of London Corporation and the Livery Companies.

The complexities of the electoral process will doubtless be fascinating for some; criticised by others and a triumph for the victors.

In the Royal Commission into London Governance in 1960 carried out by Sir Edwin Herbert it concluded "logic has its limits and the position of the City lies outside them".

Elections - a footnote:

At the annual election for Common Council members in March 2017, five members were elected who represent the Labour party

First published January 2015

I n March 2013 I wrote about Voting in the City Elections. You might wonder why I return to the subject again and this time it is personal. The elections that I mentioned in March 2013 related the regular cycle of City elections for the Common Council members. These take place every four years in March when all the Common Councilmen are up for re-election. I mentioned briefly then that Aldermen are elected every six years and that the date is set by reference to when the individual Aldermen

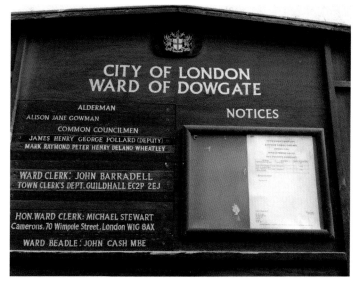

Dowgate Ward Notice Board

chose to offer themselves up for re-election - but the date must be within the six-year period. This is where it refers to me, as I had been elected in January 2009 in the ward of Dowgate and so by the end of 2014 my time was nearly up. Thus I chose to 'resign' at the end of October but indicated that I would stand again.

My earlier article sets the scene for the basis of the electorate and the arrangement of the wards in the City. Aldermanic elections have very similar arrangements to those for Common Council whereby the election is called a Wardmote and a first date is selected that might determine the outcome if there is only one candidate. However, if there is more than one then the Wardmote is adjourned to (usually) the next working day and a full 12-hour polling station is set up and votes are delivered in the usual way. There are though some variations and I will outline these in the context of my election and the general principles of Aldermanic elections.

The qualifications to be an Alderman are different to these of a Common Councilman. In order to be an Alderman you must be aged 18 years or over, a British or Commonwealth subject, an able and sufficient citizen and Freeman of the City of London and not already an Alderman of another ward. You must not be disqualified for any other reason, for example, by reason of bankruptcy or on conviction of fraud or any crime for which a prison sentence has been imposed. Also, you must either be (A) a justice of the peace on the City bench or (B) would qualify on an enhanced criminal background check similar to that needed if standing to be a Police and Crime Commissioner. Until about two years ago all Aldermen had to qualify as a JP but this was amended to the much less difficult bar of no significant criminal record. Once the Alderman has surrendered his or her office to the Lord Mayor and this is accepted at a meeting of the Court of Aldermen then the election must be held within 42 days of that surrender of office. The sitting Alderman does, however, retain office during this time.

Once you qualify on these tests a candidate needs to have five nominators who are voters in the ward to sign the nomination form. Then the election date is set and the starting gun is fired and all the usual electoral rules apply. There is a tight budget that must not be exceeded. In my ward of Dowgate where there are 411 voters the maximum that I could spend was £287.37. Not enough for a letter each and so all communication had to be hand-delivered (well it is a small ward) and printed and stuffed in basic packaging. My earlier article explains who the electors are but the added quirk in the Aldermanic election is that since an Alderman has to be a British citizen then the electors all have to be British (if you did not know, all EU citizens can vote in local elections both here and in the rest of the EU). Thus another 26 voters in Dowgate ward who are EU citizens can vote in the Common Council elections.

Dowgate Ward newsletter

In my election I was contested by one of the Common Councilmen who also represented Dowgate ward. In each ward the Alderman nominates one of the Common Councilmen to be a Deputy in the ward (a courtesy title of seniority without much substance) and it was the Deputy, Henry Pollard, who put himself forward to challenge me. You can never say never in the City but in living memory this had not happened before and so it made the election even more exciting while giving the electorate a chance to decide and not just allow a person to walk back into the role uncontested. Henry had stood for Common Council when I first became an Alderman 12 years ago and had been re-elected in the March 2013 elections that I mentioned in the opening of this article. He had had the chance to engage with the electorate more recently in relation to an election than I had. He is a member of the Skinners' Company who had not had an Alderman for over 70 years. Added to this he was supported by the other Dowgate Common Councilman.

I polished my website and prepared a plan of contact with the electorate. This would include visits in person, phone calls, emails and letter drops. I already had a good selection of contacts with all the major businesses and individuals and so used those to help with others in their firms. Anyone is entitled to a postal vote and the key is to get everyone to apply for a postal vote. Thus they can vote in their office and not need to visit the polling booth on the day. Many workers are not in the office every day and with my election being on a Friday I felt that there was more likelihood of absences for holiday business or early Christmas celebrations. In the end there were 197 postal voters registered.

What is interesting in the canvassing process is that you can really speak to people about their issues in the ward. Rubbish was a regular problem as well as roadworks and noisy building works. I had numerous meetings about demolition works taking place in the ward during this time and came out twice after 10pm to visit and hear for myself the noise and vibrations caused. I received an invite to a launch of a website by one voter and drank many cups of coffee and tea. Hospitality has to be one-way only because anything I buy for an elector would need to be recorded in the electoral expenses. One proposed meeting had to be cancelled as the company felt that it might infringe their Financial Conduct Authority registration. I must admit that I had never been in a betting office so many times before (there are two competing ones in my ward) and I might have looked suspicious as I waited for the Marks and Spencer manager to stop stacking shelves and talk to me. I made some very good and staunch allies in the process and established some true friends.

The day of the first Ward mote arrived and this was held in Dyers' Hall. This relatively small hall was kind enough to host this event and the subsequent 12-hour poll. The Ward Mote is presided over by the Lord Mayor with the City Marshal Swordbearer and Common Cryer all dressed in their finest. There were only a handful of actual voters but quite a few ringers in the audience including Murray Craig, Clerk of the Chamberlain's Court who had never been in Dyers' Hall before. The candidates are called on to make a short speech and then as there is a poll the meeting is adjourned until the morrow. From thereon I was no longer an Alderman.

On the day of the election I attended at 8am to start the long sit in the rather chilly entrance to the Dyers' Hall to await the electors in person. The staff at Dyers supplied coffee, biscuits and buttered toast to the polling clerks who sat there all day as well. Thirty-one people attended over the 12 hours and I was pleased that I had lined up a succession of friends and supporters to come along and chat to me to keep me company (but not stand in the polling station).

Once the poll closed at 8pm, the procedures were followed to record all manner of things and finally to open the votes (including the postal votes) and count them. The first three voting slips were for my opponent but then the piles evened up and the result was 101 to 18. Reader, I won.

The Lord Mayor was on call to be summoned back with the City Marshal, Swordbearer and Common

Dowgate Ward Beadle John Cash

Cryer and the Wardmote re-opened. The result was declared formally and there followed a speech each by the winner and the defeated candidate. The Dyers kindly concluded their hospitality with a bottle of champagne for the assembled supporters. The electorate had clearly indicated their wish and the Dowgate newsletter headline said it all 'Dowgate re-elects popular Alderman.'

Ward Beadles - a footnote

Each ward in the City of London has a Ward Beadle and, indeed, some have more than one because of tradition and the fact that some wards have divisions (for example, Cripplegate Within and Without). The Beadle is an officer of the ward who is nominated by the Alderman but is formally elected by the voters of the ward at the annual Wardmote (meeting of all the electors). The holder receives a nominal remuneration. Their role today is to attend with the Alderman at the various ceremonial occasions. These include the Wardmote, but also at the two Common Halls in Great Hall, the United Guilds Service at St Paul's and the formal services in St Lawrence Jewry such as that prior to the Common Hall in September electing the Lord Mayor. The most arduous role is to attend at the Lord Mayor's Show as the Beadle must be able to walk and accompany the Aldermen (riding in their coach) from the Guildhall to the Royal Courts of Justice and back again - whatever the weather. The Beadle wears a traditional great caped gown in different colours for different wards and sports a tricorn hat and white gloves. The Beadle carries the Ward Mace that is the symbol of authority of the Alderman. Many of the maces date back to the 17th century and so are precious and fragile. Beadles have traditionally been considered the Ward Constable who had to ensure that all citizens attended the meetings previously called Chief Folk-Moots and now called Common Hall. They could levy a fine for non-attendance and enforce this if need be. The Beadles have always been elected from mediaeval times and are part of the early democratic governance of the City that allowed it to flourish and thus trade so successfully.

11. THE ROLE OF THE COMMON COUNCILMAN

First Published May 2012

Common Councilman Barbara Newman CBE who wrote the article

*B*arbara Newman CBE is one of the Common Councilmen for the Ward of Aldersgate, the Ward in which Plaisterers' Hall is situated. In this article she talks about her experiences as a Common Councilman of the City of London over the past 22 years.

A small City, only 1.2 square miles divided into 25 wards and administered from Guildhall by the Court of Common Council consisting of 25 Aldermen and 100 Common Councilmen. The number of Councillors for each ward is determined by the number of electors and so varies with each ward.

In December 1989 I was elected a Common Councillor for the ward of Aldersgate where I live, one of six representing that ward. You may wonder why so many people are needed to administer such a small area but it will become clearer when I tell you that the City Corporation has more than 30 committees. This is because, as well as acting as a (very efficient) Local Authority, the City Corporation has many other responsibilities.

Among these are the ownership and management of the Barbican Centre, the Guildhall School of Music and Drama, three schools, the Old Bailey, the Veterinary Centre at Heathrow and more than 10,000 acres of open space in and around London including Hampstead Heath, Epping Forest and Burnham Beeches.

In addition to the elected members the Corporation has more than 3,000 members of staff, some based at Guildhall but many others based elsewhere in and around London. I had never been a committee person before I was elected in 1989 - the only committees I had attended were connected with my work. Indeed, it was not my idea to become a Common Councilman; I was pressed into service by neighbours when a vacancy occurred in Aldersgate. I needed to talk to my employers before making any promises

Common Council in session with the Lord Mayor arriving to preside

and secretly I hoped that they would say 'no'. They said 'yes'! Then I needed to make arrangements quite quickly to be made a Freeman of the City, one of the requirements for anyone wishing to become a Common Councilman. After that, application forms in connection with the election needed to be completed and submitted and then the all-important canvassing of the electorate, involving knocking on the doors of people who had in many cases never heard of me and stuffing paper through the doors of those who were not at home. On the day of the election there were more candidates than places and after a rather tense day and the counting of the votes I was 'in'.

My first task was to be shown around the Guildhall complex to have all the various areas pointed out in what would soon become my daily haunt including the Committee Rooms and the Great Hall in which the Council meets, all territories hitherto completely unknown to me (that is how green I was). Then the paper began to arrive, reams of it providing all kinds of information that I tried hard to absorb.

I was placed onto the Planning and Transportation and Guildhall School of Music and Drama Committees both of which were to meet early in January 1990. But first I had to be introduced to the Lord Mayor and the Common Council at their first meeting in January 1990, which I did in company with four other newly elected Councillors (interestingly only two of those are still members; the other one has become an Alderman so I am the only survivor). In those days it was the custom for new members not to speak for several months, perhaps a year, after joining the Court of Common Council, it being considered that they knew nothing and should keep quiet until they learned. As a resident of the City for several years at that time, I considered that I did know a bit and as it happened at my first ever committee meeting, of the Guildhall Music and Drama Committee, there was something on the Agenda which could adversely affect the people who had elected me to speak for them and so I disregarded custom and spoke. This upset a few of the stuffier members; but I still think I did the right thing.

The Planning and Transportation Committee is fascinating and was very busy when I joined it (I think that things are quieter just now because of the economic situation). I loved it from the first day. I was a member of the committee for 17 years and only came off when another member of my ward wanted to join it (each ward being allowed only one member per committee). It is hard work because there is so much paper to read, the brief of the Committee is very wide-ranging and of course you need to be sure you are familiar with the sites you will be dealing with which means visiting them beforehand. I remember receiving a small red plastic briefcase containing masses of documents relating to planning regulations that I needed to become familiar with. I still have the briefcase somewhere.

After about two years I was asked by other members if I would consider standing for election as Deputy Chairman at the next vacancy. I was quite alarmed at the prospect of what is a rather large job. At that time I was working full time in the City and was concerned about the time that would be involved. Once again I talked to my employers and got their agreement provided that the clients did not complain about my absence and that I made up the time. And so in January 1993 I stood for the position of Deputy Chairman and was duly elected. All went well for the first year and I learned a lot from the officers with whom I worked. Then fate stepped in, in the shape of the annual elections (now held every four years) at which the then Chairman of the committee lost his seat. The next morning early we were both due at a meeting with officers at the Guildhall and both turned up but as the former Chairman was no longer a member it was explained to him that he could not be present at the meeting. That made me Acting Chairman until the next meeting of the committee could elect a replacement. In at the deep end indeed! I was encouraged to become Chairman. After discussion with other members and my employers all was agreed and in January 1994 I became Chairman of the Planning and Transportation Committee, the first woman Chairman of that committee.

I became totally absorbed in the work of the committee and of the City Corporation generally. In April 1994 I retired from work and from then on had much more time to devote to my life on Common Council. Guildhall is a place that draws one in and whatever your interests you can find a committee that interests you because the work of the City is so varied. Before long I was spending most of the week at Guildhall.

Great Hall set up for Common Council meeting

Over the past 22 years I have served on many committees, serving as chairman of several of them and have found them all engrossing. I am presently nearing the end of my chairmanship of the Epping Forest and Commons Committee. This one meets only six times a year but because we are operating in boroughs not our own I meet regularly at the various sites with local people and organisations, including local Councillors, to tell them what we are planning for their open space and to hear from them in response. This means travelling to the different areas for meetings which usually take place in the evening but the extra time needed is I think well worthwhile and it is pleasing to hear the enormous value placed on the Open Spaces by the local people and how highly regarded the Corporation's staff are.

One of these days I will need to consider how much longer I shall go on, it is never easy to choose the right time to go. Guildhall is a difficult place to give up because one will miss the people as well as missing the feeling of being involved in something worthwhile. I shall need to give it much thought but for the moment I am too busy!

Barbara Newman CBE

Barbara Newman worked in the City for 21 years as a Trust Manager with a leading firm of City Solicitors. She has lived in the City since 1976. She was first elected to the Common Council in December 1989 and has served on many committees. Chief Commoner in 1999 and was appointed CBE on Millennium Eve 1999. She was Chairman of the Barbican Centre Committee and Deputy Chairman of the Establishment Committee in 2012 at the time of this article. Other City interests are three Livery Companies, the Royal Society of St George, the Guild of Freemen of the City of London (Senior Warden) and several Ward Clubs.

photo: City of London Corporation / Yvette Woodhouse

Canary Wharf and The City from Epping Forest

First published April 2019

The role of the Town Clerk of the City of London dates back many centuries; the first recorded holder of the office was Ralph Crepyn who held office for most of the period between 1274 and 1306. In most local authorities the role is now titled Chief Executive and the current holder styles himself as Town Clerk and Chief Executive so that it is clear how his ancient role fits in to modern local government.

Town Clerk John Barradell

It must be remembered that the City of London Corporation (of which he is Town Clerk) is a Corporation created by Charter that exercises the power of a local authority but is also a Corporation that holds lands and assets and is the City of London Police Authority and carries out numerous other functions.

The current Town Clerk and Chief Executive is John Barradell OBE. He joined the City of London Corporation in 2012 from Brighton & Hove City Council and was formerly Deputy Chief Executive of Westminster City Council. He has also spent 22 years in the private sector at firms such as Unisys and Hewlett Packard. He has served as a special constable in the Metropolitan Police and as a trustee of the Epilepsy Society.

The Town Clerk and Chief Executive of the City of London Corporation is the senior role in the City Corporation - the effective head of paid service and, as such, has authority over all other City Corporation officers as is necessary for the efficient management and execution of the organisation's functions. He is the principal advisor on matters of policy through the Policy and Resources Committee.

The Town Clerk's department is responsible for a number of areas of work, including servicing meetings of the Court of Common Council and Court of Aldermen, their committees, sub-committees and working parties. His other areas of work include taking responsibility for investigating complaints

City of London High Officers - the Common Serjeant Commissioner of the City of London Police the Town Clerk and the Comptroller and City Solicitor

Great Hall preparing for Common Council with figures representing the fallen of World War I - November 2018

against the City Corporation from members of the public, acting as the Electoral Registration Officer and being responsible for the areas of public relations, economic development and human resources. Thus while the traditional role was to ensure the keeping of records and administration of meetings - the role has now expanded greatly to oversee both the management of the extensive work of the Corporation but also to engage across London and the UK in order to ensure that the role of the City Corporation is understood at regional and national levels.

He is most visible at meetings of the Court of Common Council (the City's Council meetings) that are held in public on a Thursday lunchtime, nine times a year, in Great Hall. He sits centrally on the dais and wears a black gown, jabot and short wig. He is flanked by the other Chief Officers of the City (the City Remembrancer, Chamberlain, Police Commissioner, Comptroller and City Solicitor, City Surveyor and

Director of the Built Environment) who are on hand to deal with any issues. Seated alongside are his own Deputies and staff who keep time on any speeches and assist with any issues of debate or governance. While the Lord Mayor presides, the Town Clerk conducts the meeting, calls on Members to speak and consults with the Lord Mayor on any issues of difficulty or dispute. However, the Town Clerk also takes part in all the major ceremonies of the Civic year - swearing in the new Lord Mayor at the Silent Ceremony as well as presiding over the installation of the new Sheriffs. With others he will take part in the Lord Mayor's show, travelling in a carriage.

The work of the Town Clerk can take him outside of the Square Mile. Most notably it is worth recalling the work that John Barradell did in the summer of 2017. He is the Chair of the Local Authority Panel (LAP), which comprises chief executives who take a leadership role in resilience across London, and he is also the Deputy Chair of the London Resilience Partnership. This is a cross-London role aimed at ensuring that London is ready to confront any issues that impact locally or generally. This arrangement has been in place since the 1950s when flooding was a particular concern. Thus when the Grenfell Tower fire happened in June 2017 there was a mechanism for cross-London support. It happened that John was best placed to take on a significant role in working with the Royal Borough of Kensington and Chelsea at that time and effectively leading the response. He was supported by many staff from many Boroughs as well as staff from the City Corporation who were effectively seconded to the work in Kensington and Chelsea with its own staff for many weeks. This was largely unsung and entirely over and above John's role in the City - but it was a part of how the City Corporation can assist more widely across London both in emergency and at other times.

The Town Clerk with the Liber Albus

The most noted Town Clerk of London was perhaps John Carpenter whose time in office started in 1417 and seemingly lasted until 1438. He is famed as the author of the first book of English Common Law called 'Liber Albus'(the White Book). However, he is also well regarded as the founder of the City of London School. In 1442 he bequeathed land that was to be for the education of boys and they became known as Carpenter's children and the historic beginnings of the School, which was located at John Carpenter Street but is now on the river by the Millennium Bridge. Carpenter was a member of Parliament during his time as Town Clerk, which suggests that those two roles were a lot less demanding than the very full and exacting role of our current incumbent.

When John Barradell took the role in 2012, he said: "This is a truly unique opportunity to manage an organisation which is steeped in history at the heart of London and the nation." It is clear that he relishes this role and has embraced the history but more importantly sees the clear direction that the City must take in working for London and the UK.

13. THE CITY REMEMBRANCER

First published February 2012

A few days ago I paid a visit to Guildhall (thanks to an introduction from Alderman Alison Gowman) to see Paul Double the City Remembrancer who has held this ancient office for nearly 10 years.

Photo: The Illustrated London News

City Remembrancer Paul Double in Great Hall prior to State Banquet

The Remembrancer role dates back to 1571. Elizabeth I was on the throne. The Remembrancer is one of the City's Law Officers as well as being a Parliamentary Agent and its head of Protocol. Historically the Remembrancer is required "to continue to attend Parliament and the offices of the Secretaries of State daily and acquaint the Lord Mayor with the public affairs and other business transacted there relating to the City". This was laid down by an Order in 1685.

Nowadays Paul has regular contact with officials in government departments responsible for developing government policy, the drafting and promotion of legislation and responsibility for relations with both Houses of Parliament and Select Committees including briefings for debates in which the City has an interest. Paul attends Prime Minister's Questions and other Parliamentary debates to, as he puts it, "assess the parliamentary temperature". On the financial sector (crucial of course to the City) Paul attends Treasury questions and sends reports to Select Committees. When Paul became the City Remembrancer this part of the role had fallen a little by the wayside. He quickly established a regular parliamentary routine and presence. This can only be good for the City to ensure that its voice is heard.

How did Paul reach this important position? Well, after school in France, University in Bristol and then University College London he was called to the Bar and practised as a Barrister in general chambers at 2 Temple Gardens, which undertook Parliamentary work. Paul was instructed

Photo: The Illustrated London News

City Remembrancer and team at the Houses of Parliament

by the City Corporation to promote a bill in relation to Epping Forest. After receiving further similar instructions over several years Paul was interviewed for the position of Remembrancer.

As the City's head of Protocol, Paul's office is responsible for organising events and hospitality on behalf of the City Corporation. These include State Banquets to honour visiting Heads of State. This year, 2012, will be a vintage one with the Queen's Jubilee and the Olympic Games. Discussions with the Royal Household about the Queen's City Lunch this Summer are well advanced. There are usually two state visits each year. The planning of such visits is long in the preparation and includes holding discussions with embassies. Functions at Guildhall range from small receptions to major State Banquets and dinners to honour visiting Heads of State and Government. Related protocol and political aspects as well as business programmes, which increasingly form an integral part of the visits, are also dealt with by the Remembrancer's office in liaison with the City Corporation's Economic Development team.

State Banquet in Great Hall Guildhall in honour of the President of China with Lord Mayor Alderman Sir Alan Yarrow speaking

There has never been a more important time to get the City's message across to the widest possible number of influential people. Fellow Liveryman will be interested to know there are approximately 250 bookings each year at Guildhall, which include banquets, graduations, concerts, luncheons, receptions and gala dinners for leading British and International Companies. Paul chuckles when he thinks of the time and importance that is taken just to ensure that the seating plan at banquets is the art of diplomacy. Our learned clerk will immediately sympathise!

On the day I called to see Paul the City Corporation succeeded in its proceedings to remove the occupiers at St Paul's. Paul explained to me the difference between his role and that of the Comptroller and City Solicitor. The Remembrancer helps to frame new laws and the Comptroller applies laws that have been passed by Parliament. The Remembrancer also tracks the work of the GLA Assembly and the GLA's associated bodies.

Looking back Paul cites his work in Parliament as "a helpful presence" and the legislation that he steered through in the form of the City of London Ward Elections Act 2002 as one of his most memorable achievements. The Act permitted Companies to vote in ward elections for the first time and gives businesses in the City valuable representation.

Our City Remembrancer however is very forward-looking. He enjoys his contact with Livery Companies and assists them now and again with constitutional matters. The City is fortunate indeed to have this capable and warm-hearted man in one of its important offices.

Past Master Richard Hanney

The City's Law Officers - a footnote
The City has four Law Officers of which the Remembrancer is one. The others are the Comptroller and City Solicitor, the Recorder of the City of London and the Common Serjeant. The Recorder's pre-eminent role is detailed in another chapter. The Common Serjeant is the second senior judge at the Central Criminal Court (the Old Bailey). The office dates back to 1291 and involves not only a full role as a senior judge in criminal matters at the Old Bailey but certain duties to the City of London. The Common Serjeant plays a major role at the election of the Sheriffs and the Lord Mayor. He also presents the new Sheriffs to the Queen's Remembrancer at the ceremony of the Quit Rents. While the Common Serjeant is appointed through the usual Judicial Appointments Board process the City has representation on this Board and the Common Serjeant on appointment attends before the Court of Aldermen to take his oath of allegiance. The Comptroller and City Solicitor heads up the in house legal team of the City of London Corporation. Originally these were two roles. That of the Comptroller dates back to 1311. They were amalgamated in 1945. The in-house legal team deal with the wide variety of matters that the City is involved in from children's services to commercial property transactions. The City Solicitor is also involved in the ceremonial side of the City and also participates in the Quit Rents Ceremony. Together the four Law Officers will be called upon from time to time to opine on issues and these usually involve the custom and practice of the City as the research and joint nature of the opinion suggest that the matters can be weighty and difficult to determine.

14. THE CHAMBERLAIN OF LONDON

First published March 2016

The '80th Chamberlain of London' is a grand title for a very enthusiastic Lancastrian, Dr Peter Kane, who has been in the post for two years. He is very welcoming I found on visiting him. He works at Guildhall but he does not occupy a huge room as I had expected; rather it is functional and comfortable.

Chamberlain Dr Peter Kane

The Chamberlain of London is an ancient office dating back to at least 1237. Originally responsible for collection and distribution of revenues and appointed by the Crown, the office-holder's term traditionally began on Midsummer Day and cannot be removed 'unless some great cause of complaint appear again him'. The Chamberlain is, in modern day language, the Finance Director of the City of London Corporation. Peter enjoys the variety of his role. He is keen to ensure that the Corporation of London delivers good services to the businesses and residents in the Square Mile and that the Corporation spends its money wisely, always obtaining good value.

Peter is responsible for managing the Corporation's three key funds. The first is the City Fund, which pays for the City police service and local government activities through money it receives from central government, business rates and council tax payers. The second is City's Cash, which funds the Corporation's open spaces (for instance Hampstead Heath, Epping Forest and Burnham Beeches), cultural causes, the City's independent schools and support for training and education outside of the City. The third is the Bridge House Estates. Income was earned from tolls over London Bridge in earlier years primarily for the upkeep of the Bridge. The residue now goes to the City Bridge Trust (CBT) and is available for charitable causes. The annual amount available is circa £15 million. I shall return to the CBT later.

Peter's day is a busy schedule of meetings with senior colleagues across the Corporation and Police on financial and budget issues, particularly at this time of year when ratepayers are consulted on budget plans and Council Tax, ahead of consideration by the Court of Common Council in March. He also has to ensure that the IT is running smoothly, big transformation projects are being delivered and the City is getting a good deal from its suppliers. And he also finds time, usually early in the morning, to put his trustee hat on for a charity, Community Links, based in East London, which helps to provide advice and support to one of the poorest communities in London.

Peter exudes a sense of calmness and that of a dedicated public servant. He comes from Eccles near Manchester (he has always followed the Red Devils and cites Best, Charlton and Law as its greatest players). His parents were teachers and his two sisters (and wife) now teach too. I 'got away' says Peter with a smile.

He followed in his father's footsteps by going to Eccles Grammar School where he was proud to see his father's BSc degree and Distinguished Flying Cross (DFC) - for service as navigator in a Halifax bomber in WWII - recognised on the Honours Board. After school Peter won a place at St Edmund Hall, Oxford, where he read Politics, Philosophy and Economics and came out with a First. He then went to the LSE where he obtained a Masters in Economics and then a doctorate under Professor Steve Nickell who is a well-known economist in his field. And the international make-up of the LSE sparked a love of travelling

Chamberlain Peter Kane presides at the freedom ceremony for South African anti-apartheid heroes honoured in January 2016

which has been a great passion ever since.

After the LSE, Peter's first job was as an economist at the TUC for circa six years, preparing reports for the National Economic Development Council (NEDC) and meetings with the Treasury. Peter's next job was Chief Economic Adviser to Hackney Council, where a key priority was strengthening links with big City employers. After three years, Peter then joined the Treasury as a policy-maker with responsibility for public spending in such areas as education and local government. He was responsible for the publication of the Red Book, which sets out the government's policies and forecasts in the area of government spending. It is laid before Parliament after each budget. 'Much burning of late night oil' says Peter in the run up to Budget Day. After the Treasury Peter went to the Cabinet Office in Whitehall for three years where he was responsible for introducing public service reform and ensuring that public money was spent wisely and as carefully as possible. After the Treasury Peter served in the Home Office for seven years (under five Home Secretaries). He was Finance Director, responsible for police, immigration, passports and counter-terrorism services. He negotiated with his old colleagues for the annual grant. Again, and this is a common thread in Peter's past, he was responsible for seeing that money was spent wisely.

Two years ago Peter became the Chamberlain. He has become immersed in the Corporation with his usual enthusiasm. He admires the traditions of the Corporation and indeed the wider community in the

Chamberlain Peter Kane presides at the freedom ceremony for Sir Nicholas Winton

City. He is responsible for overseeing the awards of the Freedom of the City to distinguished recipients including the late Sir Nicholas Winton who was recognised with the Freedom in his 105th year for rescuing 700 children from pre-war Prague. Peter has personally opened Tower Bridge and driven a City of London craft underneath it.

As Chamberlain Peter plays an important role in the Silent Ceremony when the Lord Mayor is sworn into office as he presents to the new Lord Mayor the insignia of office - the Sceptre, purse and City seal. And finally the world of the Livery Companies. Peter knew little of them until recently but he admires their quiet dedication to their respective trades and their charitable activities. He also admires the way Livery Companies promote their skills to younger people and wonders whether the Livery Companies sufficiently publicise the work they do.

Peter raised the thought that the Corporation and the Livery Companies should, perhaps, be more collaborative with their respective resources. The CBT and the Livery funds are working more closely together to provide a strong financial platform for charitable giving but he wonders whether this could go further. The Chamberlain is responsible to the Court of Aldermen for constituting new Livery Companies and interpreting and amending their ordinances and charters.

Peter's advice to his eventual successor would be to respect the best of the great traditions but be ready to adapt and change to remain relevant. He is making a difference at Guildhall and in a delightfully friendly way.

Past Master Richard Hanney

The City's other Senior Officers - a footnote
The City has several other senior officers who form the senior management team of the City Corporation under the Town Clerk. The City Remembrancer and the Law Officers have already been mentioned. The City Surveyor is another such office whose role dates back to 1478. Over the years the role has been involved in the property ownership of the City in its many guises. The City Surveyor is now responsible for the City's major Central London commercial property portfolio of some 16 million square feet of space and the management of the City's 600 operational properties stretching across Greater London and ranging from the Mansion House and Guildhall to gardeners' huts in our open spaces. Other Departments of recent origin have more recognisable titles such as the Directors of the Built Environment, Children's and Community Services, Innovation and Growth, Communications, Open Spaces and Heritage, Strategic Education, Culture and Skills, Human Resources and Consumer Protection and Market Operations.

First published October 2018

The City of London has had a long link with the dispensing of justice and the Judiciary. The role of the Aldermen was to act as judges long before the Justices of the Peace Act 1361. The Sheriffs of the City of London are responsible for criminal justice and the good order of the City and pre-date the Lord Mayor dating back to the Norman Conquest. These long-standing and deep connections between the City and the Judiciary still hold true today. The Lord Mayor swears allegiance to the Queen before the Lord Chief Justice and other senior judges during the Lord Mayor's Show.

The City's copy of the Magna Carta

The relationship has a physical manifestation in that the City of London owns and maintains the three court buildings in the Square Mile - the Old Bailey, the Magistrates' Court and the Mayor's and City of London Court (exercising a civil county court jurisdiction). The Lord Mayor is the Chief Magistrate and exercises his or her right to sit at the Old Bailey to determine cases (formal matters only) during his or her year in office. That is not merely a trivial or ceremonial link - the City has frequently campaigned and promoted the importance of new court buildings - for example, the City championed the need for the Rolls Building in Fetter Lane for hearing significant international commercial cases.

The Lord Mayor promotes London and the UK as a centre of excellence for legal prowess and the rule of law that sets the UK apart from all other countries. Here our judges are incorruptible and justice is done fairly and expeditiously. Our rule of law is one of the many reasons why London is so successful as the world's most innovative, dynamic, and international financial centre. No wonder London is the centre for so many disputes, arbitrations and legal cases. The latest report shows that the revenue generated by legal activities in the UK was £31.5bn in 2016, making up 1.5% of the UK economy.

Each year in July the Lord Mayor offers hospitality to the Lord Chief Justice and senior judges as well as the Lord Chancellor at the Mansion House. This is the highlight of the year for the Judiciary to dine at Mansion House - not only can they catch up with old friends and foes but also hear the joint opinions of the Lord Mayor, Lord Chancellor (Minister of Justice) and the Lord Chief Justice.

This year the Lord Chief Justice (Lord Burnett of Maldon) did not pull any punches in this, his first speech as Lord Chief Justice. He warned that the High Court will face an 'unsustainable' shortage of judges in the coming years if nothing is done to address the current recruitment crisis. He said it was well-known there had been difficulty in attracting applicants with the right skills to fill vacancies in recent years. "There is an urgent need to act now if we are to avoid serious and lasting damage to the High Court and to the international position of the jurisdiction of England and Wales, with knock-on consequences for the professional services industry and the City," he said. Mindful that the Lord Chancellor is sitting there and is the key to better funding in order to encourage more to join the ranks of the esteemed Judiciary.

The good news that was announced was that the City of London Corporation is providing a brand new 18-courtroom facility, which will be purpose-built from scratch on the site of Fleetbank House, just off Fleet Street. The new courthouse is expected to open in 2025, subject to final funding arrangements and planning permission. The court, built in partnership with the HM Courts and Tribunal Service and the judiciary, is designed to be dedicated to courts dealing with cyber, fraud and economic crime as well as replacing the Mayor's and City of London Court and City of London Magistrates' Court (both owned by the City of London Corporation).

Lord Chancellor David Gauke said: "The flag of English law is flown in countries across the globe, and London already leads the way as the best place to do business and resolve disputes. This state-of-the-art court is a further message to the world that Britain both prizes business and stands ready to deal with the changing nature of 21st century crime."

The Lord Chief Justice added:

"The creation of this new court sits comfortably with the long overdue and much wider courts and tribunals modernisation programme…They will be state-of-the-art courts and will play an important part in the administration of justice of London. My Lord Mayor we are grateful to the City for its contribution to maintaining the rule of law and support for the administration of justice illustrated by this substantial financial commitment. With the development of Fintech, smart contracts and digital ledger technology - among other things - the establishment of what might be a bespoke financial and business court for the 21st century cannot be welcomed strongly enough."

The Lord Chief Justice also emphasised the need to uphold the rule of law:

"It is said that the judiciary are the guardians of the rule of law. That is undoubtedly true, for without an independent judiciary able to state authoritatively what the law is, and to adjudicate impartially on disputes of every nature, the rule of law would be no more than a high-minded phrase. While that

The Lord Mayor Alderman Charles Bowman with the Lord Chancellor and Lord Chief Justice, Lord Burnett of Maldon

Lord Chancellor, David Gauke MP, speaking at the Dinner to HM Judges in Mansion House

proposition is, I think, incontrovertible the judiciary cannot uphold the rule of law or administer justice in splendid isolation. The rule of law is underpinned by a partnership, with each partner playing its proper role. Parliament and the Government by statute must provide the resources, financial and administrative, necessary to maintain the courts system… The broad partnership that underpins the rule of law is reflected tonight in the three speakers. My Lord Mayor on behalf of the City and Corporation. The Lord Chancellor on behalf of the Government and Parliament and the Lord Chief Justice on behalf of the judiciary. There has been a long history of local government playing a part in the administration of justice across the nation. But the City of London through tradition and practice of long-standing is the pre-eminent example. There is a partnership between the judiciary and the City, illustrated by the dual roles of the Recorder of London and Common Serjeant as the senior judges at the Old Bailey, while

The Master Glover (the author) presents gloves to the Lord Chief Justice, Lord Thomas of Cwmgiedd, and the Recorder of London, HH Judge Brian Barker QC linking the craft with the Judiciary

also undertaking important advisory, ceremonial and community roles for the City. The City retains an interest in the Old Bailey and the Mayor's and City of London Court."

The Lord Mayor used the occasion of the dinner to praise the work of the judiciary and all lawyers. He said "Our Rule of Law is the foundation of foundations, the City of London has a series of fundamentals that make us so successful, including, among others, culture, diversity, time zone, language and a great place to live and work. But… above all… my top three fundamentals are always: number 1 - rule of law, number 2 - rule of law and number 3 - rule of law.

"First, it has made us one of the economic powerhouses of the world and has helped make London the number one international financial centre. Second, English law is the most widely used legal system: over a quarter of the world's jurisdictions have legal systems derived from ours - including Australia, Hong Kong and America. Third, it has given us the very best courts, and the City of London Corporation could not be prouder of its association with the pre-eminent criminal court, the Old Bailey. And fourth, it has given us the very best judges. And I - and the whole City of London Corporation - want to thank you for your incredible work upholding our foundation of foundations.

"And we in the City are clear that English law - and our expertise - will remain the gold standard and that the predictability, certainty and commerciality of English law will persist after we leave the EU… Brexit itself has no effect on English law."

As with all these dinners, besides the enjoyable and affable entertainment, there is a lot of serious and effective communication happening so that the necessary messages are delivered as well as appropriate thanks and positive engagement by all parties. It is because of these elements that the dinner is successful and continues to command a popular place in the legal diary.

16. THE MAGISTRACY

First published December 2011

This article is an extract of an article written for the Magistrates' Association magazine to recognise the links between the City Corporation, the Aldermen and the office of Magistrate in the City. All Aldermen are Magistrates and most sit on the City of London Bench in Queen Victoria Street. There is an historic imperative in the dispensing of justice that served to provide an orderly way of life and settled community, allowing trade and business to flourish in the City from the middle ages onwards.

The 650th Anniversary of the Justices of the Peace Act was marked in 2011 alongside the 900th Anniversary of the office of Alderman of the City of London (all of whom were, until 2013, magistrates). City of London Magistrates are proud of our remarkable heritage and its importance in the development of administering justice.

Wood Street Police Station City of London

When Edward III established the office of Justice of the Peace in 1361, he appointed Sheriffs to represent him in the counties and also chose local landowners to be Justices. The law at that time was that no man should go offensively or ride armed, before the Justices. They met four times a year to conduct their courts at Quarter Sessions. But in the medieval City of London, the Lord Mayor and Aldermen had already been functioning as Justices and Keepers of the Peace long before any charter confirmed their jurisdiction. The situation was resolved in 1444 by the charter of King Henry VI, which recognised the Lord Mayor, the Recorder and those Aldermen who had served as Lord Mayor as Justices of the Peace. This was the first in a series of charters that gradually led to the formal recognition of all Aldermen as Justices.

The first Lord Mayor's court rolls surviving from 1298 show that the court was busy punishing tavern-brawlers, bullies, nightwalkers, gamblers and other disorderly persons, as well as fraudulent tradesmen. All this will strike a chord with today's Justices! This court was to develop into the Lord Mayor's Justice Room. From 1624, the Waiting Books document proceedings that were held at Guildhall, and recorded by the Attorneys of the Lord Mayor's Court, who were effectively the first Clerks to the Justices.

The Mansion House Justice Room operated from the completion of the Mansion House in 1752. During the Gordon Riots of 1780 the House was damaged and the fear of further mob violence led to a proposal to create a side door, to prevent genteel people from having to rub shoulders with vagrants and others of low class - defendants used the grand front steps, JPs the basement entrance.

The decision to relocate from Mansion House was taken in 1986 and in 1991 the City of London Magistrates' Court moved from the Mansion House to 1 Queen Victoria Street. The Lord Mayor chaired the last bench to sit at Mansion House; his closure of that day's business marking the closure of the last court in Britain to sit in a private house. The old court room is still recognisable but now a busy office for the Lord Mayor and very few people wonder about the second door. The new location, 1 Queen Victoria Street, owned by the City of London Corporation, is itself a building of considerable historic interest. Purpose-built as one of the first safe deposits in the country, it has beneath it a huge vault - ideal for secure cells!

Today's City of London Magistrates' Court is unique in that the ancient office of the Lord Mayor includes the title of Chief Magistrate in the Square Mile. Aldermen remain an integral part of the City Bench and now sit with other Magistrates, who were first appointed in 1968.

We retain and respect our traditions. The Lord Mayor's sword stands in pride of place in Court 1, denoting his status as Chief Magistrate and under which he sits when he takes the Chair during his year of office as Lord Mayor. In 1850, the journalist George Augustus Sala wrote: "The first thing that strikes the stranger accustomed as he may be to frequenting other courts, is the unwonted courtesy of the officials, and their gorgeous costumes." Little has changed! Magistrates wear official black gowns consistent with Aldermanic tradition when sitting, reflecting the authority of the office. Some court officers continue to wear traditional 'Red Collar' uniforms.

The work of the City of London Magistrates' Court includes cases prosecuted by the City of London Police, which is a separate police force responsible for law enforcement in the Square Mile. The variety of cases brought before the City of London Justices is not only very broad, but also specialised, since the City of London Police is designated as the national lead force for fraud and economic crime. This means that the City Police bring regular requests for warrants and cash detentions under fraud proceedings as well as applications from overseas requiring information from the UK banks to be used as evidence in international proceedings.

The administrative history, being so distinct from the rest of London, is also reflected in the relationship between the City of London Court and the Central Criminal Court, the Old Bailey. The building is owned and run by the City of London Corporation. All appeals from the City Magistrates'

City of London Magistrates court

Courts are handled under the supervision of the Recorder of London and appear before City Magistrates and Central Criminal Court Judges. In addition, swearing in of all new City Magistrates takes place in Court Number One, at the Old Bailey where many of history's most notorious murder cases have been heard. It was therefore not surprising that the Lord Chancellor made special mention of the Lord Mayor's additional judicial status at the recent Mansion House banquet that the Lord Mayor gives annually to Her Majesty's Judges - an event that reinforces the ancient links of the City of London and the judiciary.

The City's resistance to the Crown's commission of the peace has not survived the modern political spirit, increasingly suspicious of anomaly and perceived privilege. By 1997 the City was assimilated into the general scheme first exemplified by the 1361 Act. Aldermen are statutorily appointed justices of the peace along with lay members, and service as a Magistrate is still considered a prerequisite for election to that office thus maintaining the connection between the civic authorities and the magistracy.*

The preservation of this important part of London's legal heritage has always been a priority for the City of London bench. As it moves on to a new role as part of the Central London Local Justice Area it will look to maintain and share its traditions with new colleagues drawn from a wider area. Once again the City of London will play its part in the continuing and evolving development of the Magistracy and in meeting and addressing contemporary challenges.†

Annie Allum and Jeff Kelly are Magistrates sitting or formerly sitting in the City of London Magistrates' Court and the Central London Bench.

* This requirement no longer applies to Aldermen
† The City of London Corporation are now working with HM Courts and Tribunal Service to relocate the Magistrates' Court at Queen Victoria Street to a new combined courts' building in Fleet Street.

17. THE RECORDER OF THE CITY OF LONDON

First published April 2014

The first Recorder of London was Geoffrey de Norton who was, by all accounts, appointed in 1298. I have been to see the current Recorder, His Honour Judge Brian Barker QC, at his office in the Old Bailey. The Recorder of London is the senior presiding judge at the Old Bailey and Brian is extremely well qualified for the role. Prior to his appointment he was the Common Serjeant of London who is second in command at 'the Bailey'.

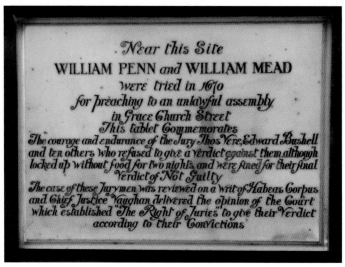

Plaque to Penn and Mead whose trial at the Old Bailey led to the determination of the rights of juries

The Recorder is appointed by the Court of Alderman of the City of London. He is involved in the formal appointment of the Lord Mayor and is also High Steward of Southwark, another ancient office, which comprises of several meetings each year of the Court Leet.

The Recorder's most important role is the administration of justice at the Old Bailey. The allocation of cases and the smooth running of the Central Criminal Court (as it is also known) is of paramount importance. Since 1971 the Old Bailey has been a Crown Court (when Assizes and Courts of Quarter Session were abolished throughout England and Wales). It has unique facilities to hear the most serious cases in the country. Approximately 75% of its cases are homicides. Thereafter some terrorist trials and cases in the public interest (such as the 'phone hacking' trials) completes its case-load. There are additional facilities for the press when public interest cases are heard.

Some of Brian's predecessors have got into difficulties. In a case knows as Penn and Mead, in 1670, the then Recorder locked up the jury for failing to convict a defendant! They remained there until being released after a writ of habeas corpus was issued by another court.

The infamous Judge Jeffreys was Recorder of London and eventually Lord Chief Justice. He was later cornered by a mob in The Prospect of Whitby Public House and died in the Tower of London.

In 1750 a fever quickly spread from Newgate Prison, which was next to the Old Bailey, and, before the outbreak was over, the Lord Mayor, two judges, one Alderman and an Under Sheriff had perished. Even to this day judges carry a small posy of flowers on ceremonial occasions to ward off noxious fumes.

In addition to his administrative responsibilities Brian sits as a full-time judge. The case before him, when we met, was expected to last six weeks.

So how did Brian reach the position of Recorder? Via Kansas and Zambia as it turned out. Brian went to Strodes School in Surrey, which has an association with the Worshipful Company of Coopers. After reading law at the University of Birmingham Brian spent two years at the University of Kansas in the US, where he obtained a Master's Degree in political science. He then returned to England and, despite advice that he should study to be a solicitor, Brian chose the Bar. "It was because I wanted to be an advocate," he says. He joined the chambers of James Burge QC and Victor Durant QC in 1 Crown Office Row in the Temple and then, after a spell in Queen Elizabeth Chambers, he finally became a Junior Tenant in the Chambers of Jeremy Hutchinson QC at 3 Kings Bench Walk. Brian practised as an

The Grand Hall at the Old Bailey

advocate undertaking common law and criminal work. As an advocate he both prosecuted and defended in the criminal courts, which, he believes, was helpful to his experience. It was at Chertsey Magistrates Court that Brian met his wife, Anne Rafferty, who has herself enjoyed a distinguished legal career. She sits as a judge in the Court of Appeal. "She works incredibly hard," says Brian. They have three grown-up

His Honour Judge Brian Barker QC robed as the Recorder of London

daughters. Of Chertsey Magistrates Court, "I haven't been back!" says Brian.

In 1990 Brian was appointed Queen's Counsel. As a senior barrister he conducted more substantial cases. He represented Kenneth Kaunda's son in Zambia. He was appointed a judge to the Old Bailey in 2000 where he has sat ever since.

Brian speaks warmly of the City of London and its traditions. He is a Liveryman and was Master of the Coopers in the same year that Ian Luder was Lord Mayor. That gave him much pleasure.

Brian told me that what really mattered to him was the administration of justice in a free society and the balance between the historical context of the Old Bailey and modern methods such as the prolific use of computers. He is passionate about the contributions made by all those who work at the Old Bailey. Everyone contributes and makes the Court a 'worthwhile institution to administer justice'.

Before meeting Brian I read some of his judgments. He has not been short of gruesome murders. What struck me was the courteous way he approaches his work in court. How fortunate we are, in the City of London, to have a great institution such as the Old Bailey with Brian Barker at its head.

Past Master Richard Hanney

The current Recorder of the City of London is His Honour Judge Nicholas Hilliard QC who has held that post since 2015.

First published 2012

The Secondary is one of those lovely job titles in the City of London that has survived since 1356. If the job description was being settled today the Secondary would probably be described as the managing director of the Old Bailey (otherwise known as the Central Criminal Court). The current Secondary is Charles Henty. To give him his full job description, he is The Secondary of London and Under Sheriff and High Bailiff of Southwark. He has been in the post since 2004.

I had previously visited the Old Bailey when Past Master Peter Cook was residing there during his time as a Sheriff. The building is one of the landmarks of the City with the unmistakable Scales of Justice

The Plaisterers' Livery visit the Old Bailey

high above. On any given day there are 380 people working in the building and 2,500 visitors including jurors and members of the public in the public galleries. Those who work at 'the Bailey' include Treasury Counsel (who prosecute for the Crown Prosecution Service), resident press, the witness service, victims' support and altogether 15 different agencies.

The Old Bailey was built, is owned and run by the Corporation of London. It is the only court owned by a local authority in England and Wales. The Secondary oversees it and ensures that it runs smoothly. It is not a job without risk. In 1972 the Old Bailey was bombed by the IRA. Who could ever forget the sight of those who were injured? Any event such as the loss of a prisoner would be reported the world over.

I met Charles Henty in his office. He is a Londoner whose father practised as a barrister in Lincoln's Inn and now lives in Sussex. His late mother was a Scot. He was educated at Eton where he became Head of the Combined Cadet Force. He then went to Sandhurst and joined the Coldstream Guards. After service in Hong Kong and Africa, Charles served in Belfast towards the end of the Troubles. Based near Belfast Charles had to deal with numerous bombings and the constant risk of death and destruction. Subsequently Charles served in Iraq, Gulf War 1, and Germany. He returned home and after considering his future Charles was encouraged to apply for the position of staff officer to the Lord Mayor of London. He was appointed in 1994.

As Head of Operations at Mansion House Charles served 10 Lord Mayors and 20 Sheriffs. He supervised inward visits and gained experience and insight into the ways and traditions of the City of London as well as the supporting business operation of the Mayoralty.

In 2004 the position of Secondary at the Old Bailey became vacant and Charles applied and was appointed. Well, if Charles is the Secondary, who is the Primary? "Oh that's my wife", is the response. Charles and his wife and their teenage children live in the West Country. Every Monday Charles leaves at 4.30am on his motorbike (he's a complete petrol head, he claims) to be at his desk to plan the week ahead. He returns home on Friday evenings. Charles and his family are accomplished skiers. I formed the view that he likes to move around at pace!

He is most definitely not a man who wastes time. Not surprisingly he is calm under pressure and can deal with the ever-present 'risk of what might happen' every working day. In the evening Charles takes groups around the Old Bailey explaining its history but there is a long waiting list.

In some ways the Old Bailey has the same problems as the Houses of Parliament. Years of under-investment has led to the need to repair and replace infrastructure such as boilers, plumbing and electrics. It is to Charles's great credit that he has negotiated the sum of £37 million to commence the biggest overhaul of the building.

Charles Henty

"I have secured this great building for at least 25 years," he says modestly but with pride. I think this is probably going to be his lasting achievement.

There is a tradition that the judges lunch together with the Sheriffs and the Secondary and invited guests. The senior judges are the Recorder of London and the Common Sergeant. High Court judges also come to try serious cases. As Charles says, "we are in the business of the most serious cases in the land, murder, rape and terrorism". The judges are highly intelligent and very hard working. "I am keen to give them privacy and the opportunity to talk whenever I can," says Charles.

Every year two new residents arrive at the Old Bailey. They are the City of London Sheriffs. During their year in office assisting The Lord Mayor, the Sheriffs live at the Old Bailey. Charles lives there too during the week.

Charles Henty is an admirer of the traditions of the City of London and the role the Livery Companies play. He is the High Court Enforcement Officer for the EC1-EC4 part of the City. Earlier this year he enforced the proceedings to remove the protesters outside St Paul's . However, Charles is left with the sad recollection of losing his brother Ed in 1993 when an enormous bomb was detonated at Bishopsgate.

The Corporation of London pays for the running of the Old Bailey. They are reimbursed to a considerable extent by the Court Service and Her Majesty's Courts and Tribunal Service, part of the Ministry of Justice.

So I asked the Secondary to tell me who else was noteworthy at the Bailey. "Oh, Matron of course" (who takes care of all who need medical help) "and Amelia Dyer". Who is she I ask? "She is one of our ghosts. She was executed in 1896." Not long ago two City of London policemen got a shock when they saw her (she is a lady dressed in white) proceeding up the main stairway.

Finally we talked about the work of the courts. Charles rarely sits in court to observe the hearings but he is moved by the sadness experienced by the families whose lives are often ruined by the events that have led to the cases being brought to court. I sense a compassionate man.

As our meeting draws to a close Charles is off to deal with new security issues. The City is fortunate to have a Secondary who is inspirational and above all a family man with a quick sense of humour. He is clearly in the right place at the right time.

Past Master Richard Hanney

First published July 2011

We, like our fellow Liverymen from all 110 Companies, owe our existence to the City of London. Over the next few months, a series of articles showing the organisation of the City Corporation and the Mayoralty and their inter-connection with the Livery will appear with the Clerk's newsletter each month.

This, the first of those articles, looks at the development of our Livery movement from the 12th to the 21st centuries, with particular reference to the past 50 years.

Master Plaisterer Tim Cooke and his Wardens July 2018

Photo: Phil McCarthy

Although it is known that Guilds existed at the time of the Norman Conquest, the oldest recorded Charter still in existence is that of the Weavers' Company dated 1155. During the next 500 years many new Guilds were formed so that by the time of the Great Fire of London, some 70 of the present day Livery Companies were already in existence. The next 250 years, a period of great social change, saw very few new Livery Companies, only eight being formed in this period.

In the past 100 years, 30 new companies have been formed all but two of these being since the Second World War.

Whereas it is relatively straightforward to see that the reason for the growth of Livery during the 12th to 17th centuries was related to trades maintaining a strong quality and commercial control over their members, it is interesting to examine the reasons for growth over the past 50 years.

This first article examines some of the reasons behind the significant growth and resurgence of the Livery movement.

Firstly, this growth was encouraged and championed by the Court of Alderman, the controlling body for the formation of new Livery Companies.

A quote from former Lord Mayor (1991) Sir Brian Jenkins who was the sponsoring Alderman for the Information Technologists Company:

"The Worshipful Company of Information Technologists was spawned by IT 82. Hence it was supported by the Government and relevant Parliamentary Committees. Keen members of the City arm of IT 82 started the journey towards Livery status in 1985. 100 founder members were invited to join from among the leaders of the industry. The initiative was well received and City company status was granted in 1987. Between 1987 and 1992 the tempo quickened. By 1998 we had a membership of 563, 58 were women, of whom five were on the Court and 32% were under 50. Livery followed in 1992 (deliberately positioned to be number 100). The Prime Minister wrote, "I am pleased to offer my congratulation on the occasion of your recognition as a livery company... this recognises the immensely important role that IT plays in industry and commerce and IT's central role in the finance and banking activities of the City of London." Margaret Thatcher had earlier written "I recognise the value of a new Livery Company to look after the interests of IT... you combine the traditions of the past with the innovation and enterprise of today."

Stained glass window of legendary but real Lord Mayor Dick Whittington in St Michael Paternoster Royal

The Company quickly assumed the role of adviser and promoter both to the City and Government, filling a significant gap.

The benefits of becoming a Livery Company were recognised by a number of professional bodies such as Solicitors, Architects and Surveyors. Although these bodies already had, and still retain, their own professional institutes, the formation of a Livery Company complemented these activities.

A quote from David Cole-Adams, former clerk to the Architects' Company:

"The Chartered Architects' Company grew out of the conviction of a number of architects who worked with, in and for the City, that their profession needed to be represented by its own Livery Company - one that could better engage with the City on design issues and environmental matters generally. Most of the 'founding fathers' were already Liverymen of other Companies and the many who have remained active have been pleased with the way that the Company has been able to play a part and in the way in which older Companies have welcomed a number of initiatives."

With the explosion of communications, the internet, and the development of the global economy, a number of companies such as the Information Technologists, the World Traders and the Security Professionals sought, and were granted, Livery status. The reasons for this are clearly stated by a former Master of the Security Professionals (one of the newest at 108):

"The Security Profession, in a number of different roles, is now seen in many if not most of the major office buildings within the City. The decision, by a number of the leading figures in the Industry to found a Guild and then work towards and achieve full Livery within nine years and to play a full part in the life of the City was an easy one - to achieve it more difficult! To find a niche to support the Mayoralty and the Corporation has led us to: Providing security briefs for the Lord Mayor prior to his overseas visits, supporting the Whittington Course to bring children from Bexley Academy and introduce them to life in the City, working with the Sheriffs setting up an annual bravery award for the blue light services and a community award and also sponsoring an annual lecture. At the same time we have embraced all the best of the older companies with support to units of the three armed services and also started to support education at the University of East London and at Reeds School."

Drapers' Livery Company coat of arms

The result of this great expansion in the number of Livery Companies has been a Livery with a much wider scope of activities, an enhanced involvement in pro bono charity activities, a demonstration of the Livery movement adapting to and moving with the times, not to mention nearly 10,000 new Liverymen.

This is the introduction to a series of articles covering our healthy Livery movement and its inter-relationship with the Lord Mayor and the City of London Corporation who are at the centre of our being.

Past Master Peter Cook

First published September 2011

Do you remember when you took the oath as a Freeman of the City of London?
It is a bit of a tongue twister but includes the promise "I will be obedient to the Mayor of this City: That I will maintain the franchises and customs thereof...."

And have you ever wondered how and why the Plaisterers exactly connect with the Lord Mayor and the Corporation of London?

Unfortunately there is a bit of "horrible" history to navigate on the way. If you are already an avid reader of the Plaisterers' yearbook or a constitutional and historical expert then you can skip this paragraph since you will know already that the City of London was from the late 12th century governed by a Mayor with Aldermen assisted by various other ward and parish constables and minor officers who ensured a regulated way of life and business. The Mayor and Aldermen regulated the Livery Companies who were then all granted a Royal Charter to exist but were all required to be accountable to the regulations of the Mayor of London. The pre-eminence of the 'Lord' Mayor and the Aldermen and Common Councilmen still exists today with the Corporation of London exercising the powers of a local authority.

Photo: Phil McCarthy

Lord Mayor, Peter Estlin at his Lord Mayor's banquet

Of course the Corporation is now itself highly regulated and controlled by Government but many of the City's other important rights and customs date back and pre-exist subsequent laws. For example, the City Remembrancer has special power to attend Parliament and acquaint the Lord Mayor with its daily business so as to ensure that the rights and safeguards of the City of London are maintained and enhanced. In almost every aspect the Corporation of London is the same but entirely different.

Historians should re-join here ... The "constituency" of the Lord Mayor is the 30,000 or so Liverymen and women who are not necessarily residents nor business occupiers in the City and indeed will come from all over the UK as well as abroad. The Lord Mayor's election is via Common Hall and "sponsored" by the Livery - albeit that the final vote is by the Court of Aldermen alone. However, the Lord Mayor is also the head of the Corporation of London - a body that is itself elected by residents and registered business voters in the City who are themselves not necessarily members of any Livery. Thus it becomes clear (or even more muddled) as to how the bodies interlink and cross over and how the Liveries are closely involved with the Corporation but distinct from some of its important local authority remit. It may be controversial to suggest (but it is a legal possibility) that the Corporation of London could survive without a Lord Mayor. It might then look a bit more like - or be subsumed within - the London Boroughs of Tower Hamlets or Islington.

But while there is a Lord Mayor, the Government of the day has seen the importance of using the unique and significant importance of the role that the Lord Mayor can perform in a non-party political way on behalf of the UK. The physical proximity of the Lord Mayor within the heart of the financial city and the connection with the Corporation of London of which he or she is an elected member means that the Lord Mayor can engage with the business leaders and work with them and for them as the UK ambassador for financial services. This has been built up over the recent decades to a pre-eminent part of the Lord Mayor's role. It works well because of the interaction between the business voters who are the electors and stakeholders within the Corporation and also the businesses that want to have their issues aired on a national and international front and want the Lord Mayor to act as their spokesperson on such a platform. In many cases Livery Companies are engaged with this part of the Lord Mayor's work. The Financial Services Group of Livery Companies frequently brief the Lord Mayor on financial matters.

The City of London and the Millennium bridge

The Lord Mayor has thus been able to enhance the reputation of UK financial services and the City of London as a place of excellence to work and do business. The Lord Mayor promotes both the value of the City as a cluster of like businesses, a well regulated and fairly taxed environment, a place with qualified and available staff and an enjoyable environment in which people will enjoy doing business and living.

It must be remembered that although UK financial services and, especially, the banks have come under much critical scrutiny over the last few years, the financial services sector provides jobs for over one million people within the UK economy (approximately 480,000 in the City of London) and contributes 11% of the UK Government tax receipts.

The Corporation of London's role as a local authority is also vital since it is that body which ensures the physical environment is well presented, that transport runs on time (at various times the Corporation has funded alternative bus or river taxi facilities while underground lines were out of order), it has campaigned for Crossrail and is making a substantial contribution to its cost. The Corporation ensures that services such as waste collection, road cleansing and maintenance are exemplary and facilitate the planning of appropriate buildings that facilitate both large and small businesses in operating successfully within the City environs.

The Livery Companies have a lot to contribute and in many different ways - as voters and stakeholders with the City Corporation as its local authority; as part of the constituency of the Lord Mayor in the Shrieval and Mayoral elections; as business people ready to engage in the promotion and future of the City of London. Let us all Freemen and Liverymen deliver on that promise.

21. THE LIVERY COMMITTEE

First published November 2011

The first mention in archival papers of a Committee of the Livery was in 1782, but the forerunner of the present Livery Committee began on July 4th 1864. It was originally established with the following brief "The Committee is to consider the best means and take such measures as they deem advisable for securing the Guildhall from the intrusion of strangers at the meetings in Common Hall". The Committee has undergone several reincarnations in the intervening nearly 150 years, and notably the role of the Committee was amended in 1942, with a widening of its terms of reference, "To consider any matters affecting the interests of the general body of the Livery and to report recommendations at the ensuing Common Hall."

And thus it is today, with its two principal purposes - to oversee the arrangements for Common Hall: at the Election of Sheriffs on Midsummer Day (June 24th) and the Election of the Lord Mayor each Michaelmas Day (September 29th). And to act as the conduit for communication between the livery (and its masters, prime wardens, courts, liverymen and clerks) and the "powers that be" at Guildhall (including the Chamberlain's Court), Mansion House, and the Old Bailey, on any matter affecting the interests of the general body of the Livery. The committee is also now a means of improving communications between the Corporation and the Livery, increasing the involvement of Liverymen in City affairs, and acting as a forum for discussion.

The Livery badge of office worn by the Chairman and kindly donated by Past Chairman and former Sheriff Geoffrey Bond OBE

Between 1981 and 2002, these roles were split between the Livery Committee (the former), and a Livery Consultative Committee (the latter). But by a resolution of Common Hall on June 24th, 2002, the two were merged to form the presently constituted Committee, consisting of two Alderman, six Common Councilmen, six Clerks of Livery Companies, and six Liverymen who are not on Common Council. The allocation of committee places to liverymen and clerks is laid down to ensure representation between the Great 12 companies, the Clerks' Association companies (ie those with Halls, eg the Plaisterers), and the Fellowship of Clerks companies (broadly, the rest).

Members are elected for a term of three years, and may stand for re-election once (ie to serve a total of six years). Ultimately members are elected by Common Hall, but the nominations are put forward by the three Clerks' associations mentioned above (and also by the Courts of Aldermen and Common Council). Any liverymen wishing to put their name forward should do so through their company clerk.

The committee meet three times a year (in February, June and September), and additionally at the two Common Halls. The Chairman and Deputy Chairman are elected annually (at the September meeting) and typically serve a maximum of three years (if re-elected). The convention is that the chair alternates between a Common Councilman and a liveryman.

Nigel Pullman Past Chairman and former Sheriff and author of the article

But recent experience has shown that the time bar of six years has meant there can be a shortage of committee members with the experience to take on the chair without over-running their time on the Committee. For this reason, at Common Hall in October 2011, it was resolved that time spent in office (as chairman or deputy) would not count towards the six-year maximum. The Clerks do not take the chair, nor the deputy chairmanship.

Livery Masters parading to service in Guildhall Yard in order of precedence - juniors first

Much of the Committee's work is done through its two Working Groups (WG). The Communications WG is responsible for all training courses and briefings - namely the City Briefings, Wardens & Court Assistants' Course, Clerks' Briefing, and Masters' After Dinner Speaking Course. The latter three are arranged annually, but there are four City Briefings each year, and if you are reading this and haven't attended one - speak to your Clerk!

The second, the Livery Companies WG consider, among other matters, best practice amongst the Companies (while always recognising the sovereignty of each company), and appoint each member of the Committee to be the liaison member for up to eight livery companies.

The Livery Committee, though administered at Guildhall, is not a committee of the City of London Corporation, and hence has some autonomy. However, this may also mean some limitations as to its power, and so it largely works by influence and consultation. It has included the following in its brief:

"To assist Livery Companies in their support of the Mayoralty and the Corporation.

"To create awareness amongst Liverymen and the general public, especially opinion formers, of the work of the Livery Companies in their trade, professions, educational, community support programmes and charitable activities.

"To undertake such other tasks which are intended to be in the best interests of the general body of the Livery."

Nigel Pullman
Chairman, Livery Committee 2013-16 and liaison member for the Plaisterers' Company.
Sheriff of the City of London 2012- 2013

The current Chairman of the Livery Committee is Victoria Russell who is a Past Master of the Arbitrators' and Constructors' Livery Companies.

First published July 2012

At the Diamond Jubilee celebrations, the City Livery Companies were given the honour to host a lunch for Her Majesty the Queen in Westminster Hall. Many Livery Masters attended and brought with them, as their own personal guests, representatives of the schools, charities and military units whom they support. This gave the widest possible mix of backgrounds, ages, crafts, professions and organisations. The Master Mercer was given the unenviable job of addressing the audience at the end of the lunch. He very succinctly stated:

The Duchess of Cambridge enjoying herself in the Company of the Master Glover and Master Pattenmaker in Westminster Hall

"From the City's Livery Companies; a little like the Monarchy, we cherish our great history and we have a continued commitment and engagement to meet the demands and challenges of the modern age, and from the causes and the people across the nation we are proud to support."

He concluded: "It is my honour to speak for the City's Livery Companies today, but I do so with a voice of countless millions raised alongside my own. God Save Your Majesty!"

In his short allotted time the Master Mercer was able to encapsulate the objectives and work of the Livery Companies and to use that platform to speak on behalf of so many.

The Livery Companies do not always get an easy or clear message to the press and public. Thus I am pleased to be able to share with the Plaisterers the lecture given by the Lord Mayor, as part of the Gresham College programme, entitled "What Has The City Ever Done For Us".

The Lord Mayor was answering the question raised by the world at large about the City's apparent elitism and financial security and used the opportunity to explain the work and rationale of the Livery Companies. The hall held some 150 people but the lecture is available online via the Gresham College website and is expected to reach a significantly larger audience. The Gresham website receives over one million downloads per annum. In particular, I would like to précis the following elements from the Lord Mayor's lecture but also urge you to view the audio or download the script for further and fuller edification.

The Right Honourable the Lord Mayor, Alderman David Wootton, said:

"Our City Livery companies …. operate in this way - with targeted gifts, designed to serve specific needs - for a sustained period of time. And make a real difference for the future. The Building Crafts College in Newham, supported by the Carpenters' Company, is providing skills, aspiration and hope to young people from a community with high unemployment. The skills they gain will help build up this community and contribute to the Thames Gateway regeneration for decades to come.

"In 1907, Lord Mayor William Treloar founded an Appeal for children with non-pulmonary tuberculosis - building a hospital and school with support from the Livery. Over 100 years later Treloars is one of the most advanced, specialist schools for disabled children in the world - and its enormous costs are still met with significant help from the Livery…

"This year, I have seen many projects spring up in support of young people and sport - spurred on by the London 2012 Olympic and Paralympic Games. I hope these initiatives will be part of a lasting legacy beyond the Games - inspiring and investing in many more young sportsmen and women. But I also have

Lord Mayor Alderman David Wootton

real admiration for those who invested in the years building up to the Games - such as the Great 12 Livery Companies, who have identified and supported promising young athletes for many years…

"This sort of intervention may not even occur to many of us. But thanks to those who are using their particular knowledge of particular needs - making their giving as effective as possible, and enhancing monetary gifts with practical action - we are seeing real results. In this instance, several athletes made such startling progress that they have either qualified for, or are on the edge of, the British team.

"The Livery are an enormous force for good - a responsibility borne for hundreds of years. They are the living embodiment of connections in the City. Championing their professions, trades and crafts - often with roots deep into the regions - and forming a network across every sector of business and the City. And they do a huge amount to support people into education, employment and training, as well as initiating and funding a broad spectrum of charitable projects. I could spend the entire day listing their many successes. And the many ways in which we have all benefited from their quiet, yet immensely powerful, support!

"The Livery Companies are a microcosm of the City. They are not involved directly in manufacturing, but they make important and valuable contributions to the manufacturing sector - through investment in their trades and crafts. Crucially, through bursaries, apprenticeships and award-schemes - which ensure that these skills are preserved and passed on for the future.

THE NATIONAL SERVICE

of

THANKSGIVING

TO CELEBRATE

THE DIAMOND JUBILEE

OF HER MAJESTY THE QUEEN

ST. PAUL'S CATHEDRAL

Tuesday 5th June 2012

10.30 am

Order of Service at St Paul's for the service of Thanksgiving to Celebrate the Diamond Jubilee

The Lord Mayor greets the Duke and Duchess of Cambridge at the service at St Paul's Cathedral

"This long-termism, whereby funding is maximised through mentoring and other practical, 'hands-on' support, is sowing a seed for the future.

"I am delighted that the Livery was at the heart of celebrations of Her Majesty's Diamond Jubilee - out in force at the lunch for Her Majesty at Westminster Hall. Eighty-five Liveries were represented, and 530 of the guests - four-fifths of everyone there - were members of the charities, schools, trades, crafts and uniformed services which the Livery supports.

What a testament to the priorities and meaning of the Livery. With roots in medieval times, the Livery - the Guilds - have nurtured their industries through education, training and mentoring."

The full lecture can be viewed and downloaded at www.gresham.ac.uk

First published February 2017

The City of London is the oldest continuous municipal democracy in the world and pre-dates Parliament. Have you ever wondered exactly how that governance was established? The City's constitution is rooted in the ancient rights and privileges enjoyed by citizens since before the

Charter to the City of London of King William 1067

Norman Conquest in 1066. Before William I arrived the City and its citizens already enjoyed certain rights, privileges and laws and had done since the time of Edward the Confessor (1042-62). Even before that in Saxon London the municipal authority rested principally with Aldermen ('elder' men or elderfolk), who met in the City's ancient Court of Husting - the supreme court of the medieval City, with administrative and judicial functions. There is reliable evidence of its existence in 1032, although it was probably much older, and by the mid-12th century it was held weekly. It is likely that the Court of Aldermen developed from the administrative side of the work of the Court of Husting.

But returning to the arrival of William in England (after the Battle of Hastings that was so well remembered in 2016), we need to see how his rule and acceptance as King was also the start of the written evidence confirming the power of the City of London. When William arrived outside London he found the people hard to subdue and although he might have fought them it would have been a hard battle. Instead he sought a compromise and détente. It was key to how William won the support of London and how the City itself began to gain its special autonomy.

All this is contained in a small but iconic piece of vellum - the "William Charter" - the oldest document in the City's archive and given by William I to the City in 1067, soon after the Battle of Hastings, but before he entered the City of London. It has been in the City's keeping continuously ever since. It measures just six inches by one and a half with two slits, the larger one used as a seal-tongue and the other as a tie. The seal impression, although detached and imperfect, is one of the earliest surviving examples from William's reign.

Charter with seal

The Charter is written in Old English (and so, notably, not in William's native Norman French) and in the form of an administrative letter, a style commonly used by early English kings. Translated into modern English, it reads: "William King greets William the Bishop and Geoffrey the Portreeve and all the citizens in London, French and English, in friendly fashion; and I inform you that it is my will that your laws and customs be preserved as they were in King Edward's day, that every son shall be his father's heir after his father's death; and that I will not that any man do wrong to you. God yield you."

The document reflects William's recognition of the importance of London, and its concentration of trade and wealth, which he wished to safeguard. After defeating the English army under Harold Godwinson at the Battle of Hastings in October 1066, William brought his forces on a slow and marauding march north, subjugating towns along the way, before forming an encampment at Westminster. He threatened to besiege and ransack the City, where many of the remaining leading men of the Anglo-Saxon court had congregated, and the subsequent peaceful surrender, for which the Charter was a reward, was good for both sides. It was issued soon after William's coronation in Westminster Abbey on Christmas Day 1066, and was a key means whereby he won the support of Londoners; the degree of autonomy which it guaranteed has been valued and defended by the City ever since. The Charter also reflects London's already established international character by addressing both the French and English residents and treating them with equal status.

King William I

It is especially significant not only for its survival, but also because it is the earliest known royal or imperial document to guarantee the collective rights of the inhabitants of any town (it is not directed to specific groups, such as merchants, or to institutions such as major churches). The Charter granted nothing new to the Londoners, but confirmed the citizens' rights and privileges already in existence. One of the primary concerns of Londoners, as expressed in this charter, was to ensure that the succession to property was not subject to arbitrary royal intervention.

The document is one in a long line of charters that the Citizens of London extracted from the Sovereign; there are over a hundred royal charters in the City's archive (thus lots of anniversaries and articles still to be written). In 2010 the document was inscribed in the UNESCO United Kingdom Memory of the World Register, an online catalogue created to recognise documents of outstanding national cultural significance, and to support and raise international awareness of archives and their importance.

It is taking centre stage now and will be on display at the City of London Heritage Gallery from 7 January to 27 April 2017. The City Heritage Gallery is a relatively newly created space just at the bottom of the stairs of the Guildhall Art Gallery as you approach the cloakrooms.

It is rare for this document to be on display but the City could not miss marking the 950th anniversary of its grant.

The City's archives are extensive. This year will see a series of displays and events celebrating the history of the archives, which hold some three million files, covering London and Londoners from the Normans to the present day. Geoff Pick, the director of the archives, says rightly that they are arguably the best held by any city in the world.

First published 2011

*A*ll Liverymen are also freemen both of the Company but also of the City of London. There is still a great mystique to this privilege and the Clerk to the Chamberlain's Court, Murray Craig unpacked some of the history and importance of this as he lectured on this topic at Gresham College recently.

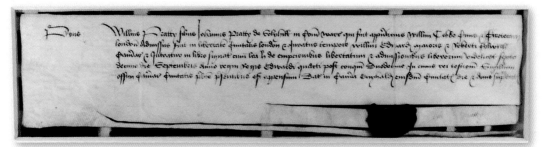

Oldest known freedom certificate dated 1472 granted to William Pratty a Glover, who became a Leatherseller in 1502

Can you take sheep over London Bridge?

The answer is no because the City of London Police are not keen on this custom in the 21st century. This is not altogether surprising because a herd of sheep, in addition to the buses, taxis, and commuters crossing London Bridge, would cause absolute traffic chaos! In the past you had to pay a toll for taking sheep across the bridge. You would be taking the animals to the Wool Exchange or Smithfield Meat Market for sale and not paying the toll would considerably enhance your profit margin. You could take cattle, pigs, hens, ducks, geese - indeed any livestock over the bridge and not pay the tariff but in the medieval period the sheep was queen of the beasts because the wool and cloth trade was the bedrock of the English economy. It is said that because more sheep went over the bridge than any other animals put together that the bridge was built and maintained on the back of sheep.

So what of other privileges?

Freemen could be hanged with a silk rope if they committed murder or treason; they could wander around the City with their swords drawn to defend themselves from footpads; they were exempt from the tender mercies of the press gang because as Freeman and skilled craftsmen, they were far too valuable to be carted off to sea. Freemen were allowed to be drunk and disorderly and granted safe passage home from the Watch. Sadly none of these privileges are available today. The main remaining privileges are of a charitable and educational nature. For example, a widow could go the Freemen's Almshouses and an orphan could go to the Freemen's School without paying a fee. There is also a Christmas fund for impoverished Freemen that pays 75 pounds 10 shillings and sixpence.

What is the Freedom?

The Freedom of the City of London is very ancient indeed. We think that the first recorded Freeman was in 1237. Today the Freedom is largely symbolic and represents a unique slice of London's history. However, in the Middle Ages it was a very valuable working document in that it was the right to trade. It would enable you to carry out your trade or craft as a member of one of the venerable City of London Livery Companies. However, there were two catches - one was the fee which was much higher than the relatively small £25/£30 fee today which I hasten to add does not swell the coffers of the City Corporation but goes to the Freemen's School for the Foundation Scholarships. The second catch was that the Lord Mayor and the City expected that the Guild would maintain quality and excellence in the goods and services provided. This worked for centuries until the Victorians came along. They did not like monopolies and

Freedom party for the Mayor of the Royal Borough of Greenwich, Peter Brookes with City supporters

cartels. They liked laissez-faire and free trade. So the requirement that you had to be a member of a Livery Company to be a Freeman was lifted and in 1835 the Freedom was widened to incorporate those living or working in the City as well as those who were members of the Livery Companies.

Obtaining the Freedom

This can be done in a number of ways mainly by redemption, ie payment. One has to apply for the Freedom either by a Livery Company or by nomination whereby an application form should be completed. The first stage is an application interview where the relevant paperwork is submitted. Stage two is the ceremony. This is a formal affair. The recipient and guests are greeted and ushered into the Court Room by the Chamberlain's Court Beadle. He announces them to the Clerk of the Chamberlain's Court who invites them to step forward and read aloud the declaration of a Freeman.

The recipient is then invited to sign the Freedom's Declaration Book and the Clerk then presents the recipient with the copy of the Freedom Certificate, which is written by the Court Calligrapher on sheepskin parchment. In addition the recipient is presented with The Rules for the Conduct of Life, which was written by a former Lord Mayor of London, Sir John Barnard, in the early part of the 18th century for the benefit of wayward young apprentices. The Clerk then extends the right hand of fellowship and greets the new Freeman as a citizen of London.

Despite being a solemn affair the ceremony occasionally has some humorous moments, for example, in the variety of renditions made. Some people read it very quietly and some read it very LOUDLY. A learned priest once read it in Latin but recently I heard the best ever rendition, which was given by Dame Judi Dench who read it in the style of Lady Macbeth, M, Desdemona and Queen Victoria combined!

Legal Aspect of the Courtroom

Historically the Court used to have a legal function in that it was a Court of Arbitration to resolve

Freedom party for the Alderman elected by the Hamburg Morgensprache - honouring a Hanseatic link to the City of London

disputes within the Livery Companies. It could be that the apprentice was not reading the terms of his indentures and was drunk, idle, indolent, staying out all night, being away from work, producing shoddy workmanship or making merry with the Master's daughter! However, it might be the Master who was transgressing. He might have beaten the apprentice, locked him in a garret or worse still did not pass on the skills and mysteries of being a Skinner, Haberdasher or Merchant Taylor. So whether or not Master or apprentice appeared before the Clerk (who had similar powers to the Judges of today) there may be a stern word, a fine, or in extreme cases they may be dispatched to the Bridewell lock-up for 14 days on a diet of bread and water! Freemen are often worried at this stage but the last case was in 1917.

Honorary Freeman

The Honorary Freedom is the highest award that the City can bestow on an individual citizen. It is a much more modern phenomenon than the 'economic' freedom that dates back to the 13th century. The first Honorary Freedom was King Charles II in 1674. It is interesting to note that he is the only reigning monarch to have it granted as it is customary to grant it to children of the monarch. Following Charles II there were only two other Honorary Freedoms until 1757 when Pitt the Elder received the Freedom. From that year on, there has been a steady flow of Honorary Freemen. The Honorary Freedom is a ceremony of much pomp and pageantry usually held in the Great Hall before full Court of Common Council and invited guests. Recipients receive a specially illuminated copy of Freedom together with a gold box to the value of 100 guineas. Recipients are a roll-call of British history and include Pitt the Younger, Nelson, Wellington, Disraeli, David Livingstone, Kitchener of Khartoum, Florence Nightingale and Winston Churchill. The latter was given the Honorary Freedom in 1943 during the height of the Second World War. He was not given a gold box but a wooden one made from timber salvaged from the Blitz in 1940.

Last year, 1,685 people were admitted to the Freedom of the City of London. This sounds like a lot of admissions but when you think there are 108 different Livery Companies in the City of London and if each of them send a dozen people each year, you can see how the numbers add up. It is a gratifying thought that the Chamberlain's Court is as busy today as it was in the 17th to 18th century.

©Murray Craig, Gresham College 2011

First published October 2014

All members of the Livery are Freemen of the City and we have all enjoyed the short but meaningful ceremony.

On September 24th 2014 the City bestowed the Honorary Freedom on Sir Tim Berners-Lee. This saw a lot of press coverage. It is the highest honour that the City can bestow on anyone. You cannot apply to become an Honorary Freeman; you have to be asked by the Court of Common Council, which formally passes a resolution confirming this.

The ceremony takes place on a much grander scale than you have experienced in the Chamberlain's Court but is basically the same ceremony and tongue-twister oath. It will often take place in the Great Hall of Guildhall although the last one (for Archbishop Desmond Tutu) took place in Mansion House. The event is effectively a meeting of the Court of Common Council before the Lord Mayor the Aldermen and the Court of Common Council. Other invited guests will attend but not the general public.

Rather than Murray Craig (the Clerk to the Chamberlain's Court), the Chamberlain himself will preside. As a new Chamberlain, (Peter Kane took over earlier this year) the ceremony for Sir Tim will

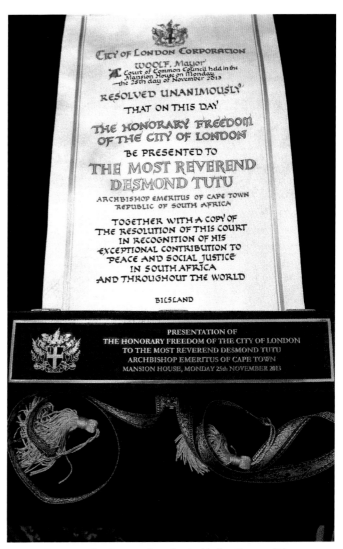

Honorary Freedom certificate for Archbishop Desmond Tutu

be Peter's first high-profile and formal event. A citation of the reason for the honour is read aloud to the assembly. The oath is administered and the new/youngest Freeman is presented with his or her freedom on an illuminated scroll. There are copies of these individual freedom documents on the walls of the Chamberlain's Court - Lord Nelson, Mrs Thatcher and Princess Diana among them. Traditionally, the scroll is presented in a silver (formally gold) box. This would be embellished with the City's coat of arms and similar insignia. Florence Nightingale was awarded the honour when she was 88. A previous bar on women being eligible had been lifted. She eschewed the usual gold box and asked for a simple wooden one. The item provided by the City is an ornate box with Crimean battles illustrated on it and actually still on display in the Chamberlain's Court. There is nothing simple in the City.

The youngest Honorary Freeman signs a special book kept only for Honorary Freemen. It is a treasure trove of important international people over the past 100 years or so. They are expected to make a formal response and speak of the honour bestowed and expound on their work that led to this event or perhaps, their love of London. With luck a lunch or dinner follows and there are likely to be more toasts and speeches.

Painting showing the ceremony for Winston Churchill

The more recent recipients, at whose ceremonies I have been present, have been Nelson Mandela, Helmut Kohl, the Duke and Duchess of Gloucester (jointly) and Archbishop Desmond Tutu, who told the story of how, when he first came to London in the 1950s, he would frequently ask Police Officers the time as he was tickled to be called Sir by a white man.

Lord Nelson so enjoyed the Banquet after his Honorary Freedom that when he won another important victory he asked the City to award him the Freedom again. They declined but did give another Banquet in his honour.

Princess Diana was told by the Lord Mayor that as a Freeman she could, if times got hard, apply for a place at the City's almshouses in Brixton. (Note to speech-writer… !)

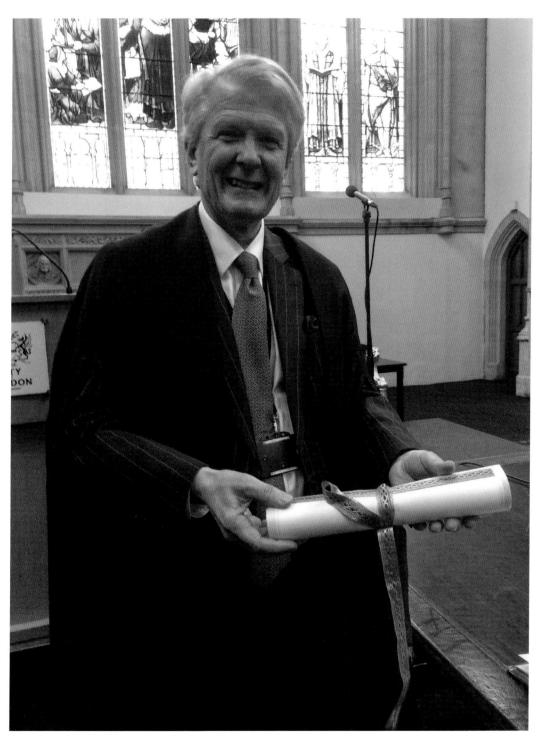

Clerk to the Chamberlain's Court, Murray Craig, with the scroll for an Honorary Freeman

First published November 2016

Everyone knows about the Lord Mayor's Show, when the Lord Mayor proceeds to the Royal Courts of Justice in order to make a declaration before Her Majesty's Judges that he/she will be faithful to the Queen and carry out the important duties of Lord Mayor.

However, it is on the day before, at the Silent Ceremony, that the Lord Mayor actually takes up office in a very moving and almost private ceremony. It is not a formal Common Hall to which all Liverymen are summoned and, indeed tickets are hard to come by (apply online and keep your fingers crossed). The setup is in itself very special with the ceremony performed not on the dais but in the body of the

General view of Great Hall and the silent ceremony

Great Hall and with lights dimmed to give further focus and meaning to the purpose of the Lord Mayor making an oath and receiving the insignia of office.

Prior to the ceremony, held at 3pm on Friday (the day before the Lord Mayor's Show), the Lord Mayor, Lord Mayor Elect, Aldermen, Chief Officers of the Corporation and friends and family of the Lord Mayor Elect lunch at Mansion House and a farewell speech is made by the outgoing Lord Mayor in a very sombre manner. All arrive at the Guildhall in time to process from the Court of Aldermen at 2.55pm precisely. The Aldermen are attired in violet gowns (trimmed with bear fur). It is with a slower and more deliberate march that they enter into Guildhall, the spurs of the City Marshal clicking on the marble flags. The procession is formed with the Officers followed by the Aldermen (juniors first) and accompanied by their Beadles. The seating is arranged with the Lord Mayor in the centre behind a table and with the Aldermen seated in an oval running away from him(her) on either flank. On his/her right the Recorder and on the left the Lord Mayor Elect.

In total silence the Common Cryer is the first to move and approaches the table with the City's Mace on his shoulder. Once there, the Cryer makes three reverences to the Lord Mayor and then brings the Mace to rest upright and balanced on the floor. The Town Clerk approaches the table and makes three reverences and then reads the statutory declaration to the Lord Mayor Elect who, standing, repeats this and then signs his/her name to the oath (alright so not entirely in silence!). The outgoing Lord Mayor then surrenders his/her seat to the incoming Lord Mayor and they reverse places. The outgoing Lord Mayor takes off his/her hat as the incoming Lord Mayor puts on his/her hat. It has been determined that this is the moment at which power passes.

A series of Senior Officers of the City of London Corporation then approach the new Lord Mayor making in each case three obeisances and presenting the insignia of office and making three further obeisances as they retreat. The Lord Mayor and outgoing Lord Mayor stand to receive them and the outgoing Lord Mayor touches each item as it is then notionally handed to the Lord Mayor. The Chamberlain brings the Sceptre first and it is placed on a velvet cushion in front of the Lord Mayor. The Chamberlain then brings the Seal of the office of mayoralty and finally the Purse.

The Swordbearer advances with three reverences and presents the Sword of office and the Common Cryer does the same with the Mace. The Swordbearer then brings the collar of esses (only being part of the ceremony since 1976).

The items presented by the Chamberlain are then all removed by the Principal Clerk to the Chamberlain. The Swordbearer and Common Cryer remove the items that they presented - all of them making three further reverences as they walk backwards to find their correct places and not missing their footing.

The Comptroller and City Solicitor then advances with three reverences and presents the indenture of the City Plate (silver and gold items kept in the Plate room under lock and key at the Mansion House) and the agreement

The Insignia of Office presented to the new Lord Mayor by the Chamberlain of London - the sceptre, seal and privy purse

for the payment to the incoming Lord Mayor of an allowance in lieu of any fees for carrying out the role of Lord Mayor. The Lord Mayor signs this.

The Remembrancer then advances with three reverences and presents the Lord Mayor with the appointment of the Deputy City Gauger which the Lord Mayor signs.

The Aldermen, Recorder, Sheriffs, Officers Chief Commoner and members of the Lord Mayor and Sheriffs' Committee in rotation greet the new Lord Mayor in a parade akin to a slow dance movement around the table and return to their respective seats. All still silent.

The Lord Mayor with the outgoing Lord Mayor followed by the orderly Aldermen and Beadles with the Officers then leave the Guildhall. A fanfare of the State Trumpeters of the Household Cavalry is sounded to herald the new Lord Mayor. The bells of St Lawrence Jewry begin to ring. Some photos may now be taken but soon the Lord Mayor enters the mayoral car (LMO) and takes the seat on the right-hand side with the outgoing Lord Mayor on the left (a reverse of how they arrived). The Swordbearer will also be present in the car. At this point the outgoing Lord Mayor is handed, by the Swordbearer, the Key to the City Seal and Hospital Seal, which the outgoing Lord Mayor gives to the new Lord Mayor. The new Lord Mayor returns it to the Swordbearer for him to keep in the fold under his wonderful fur hat.

The Silent Ceremony has been enacted for many centuries. Sometimes called the "silent change", it is perhaps a testimony to the seamless way that each new Lord Mayor continues the tradition and work that has gone before and the City's highest office is renewed.

The City Sceptre

First published December 2018

While many have heard of (if not attended) the Lord Mayor's Banquet, not many have heard of nor attended the Lighting Up Dinner. This is in effect a trial run for the Banquet.

Why such an event is necessary involves an interesting historical diversion which then leads to a description of the very enjoyable evening of October 30th 2018 as a prelude to this year's Lord Mayor's Banquet.

The holding of the Lord Mayor's Banquet (historically on the same day as the Show itself, but no longer) dates back to the early part of the 16th century. However, it was not until 1777 following a few years in which the banquet had not been conducted with "the decorum becoming this great City" that a committee was set up to superintend the banquet and this is the origin of the Lord Mayor's and Sheriffs' Committee.

The State Trumpeters practice in mufti

The terminology of this Lighting Up Dinner already suggests that the dinner has something to do with the lighting of the venue so let us understand what the arrangements were. In 1791 the contractor fitting out the Guildhall undertook to provide 6000 glass lamps of various colours, 800 back lanthorns and 15 dozen pounds of wax candles together with a sufficient quantity of cotton spermaceti oil. The lamps needed to last from 4pm on the day of the show to 4am the next day. It does not recall if the Worshipful Company of Lightmongers had a role to play in this extravaganza. Think extreme Christmas tree lights!

However, it seems that the Lighting Up Dinner specifically dates from when wax gave way to gas. This allowed more flare in the design and the effect was to beautify the Guildhall with displays of artistic merit as well as illumination. It was first lit by gas in 1815 and proved a success. Even the actual process of lighting became a popular event for people to come and watch. But the change from candles to gas did not lessen the concern about the safety of the event. In 1827 an incident occurred at the Banquet when a board of lights showing a large anchor dislodged from the east window and fell with a great crash on to the Lord Mayor and Lady Mayoress below. The Lord Mayor, Alderman Matthias Lucas, was cut about the head and several guests including the Duke of Clarence also received wounds. The Lady Mayoress escaped physical injury but the oil from the lamps ruined her dress. The Clerk of the City's works, William Montague, was held responsible because he had not checked the apparatus (the allegation was that he refused to go up the ladder for £500). He had therefore failed to notice that the fixings were poor and the wood was unseasoned and likely to warp in the heat. The image is of that dinner with the anchor and the dramatis personae being overlooked by Gog and Magog shouting a warning! Thus in 1828 it is recorded that the Lord Mayor's and Sheriffs' Committee accepted an offer from the Norwich Union to provide 18 firemen on the night.

Although the Guildhall is now well lit by electricity and is fully health and safety compliant a sense of concern and of the need to check things still permeates the Lighting Up Dinner. But in true City tradition more ceremony has been added to help people fully enjoy the event.

The Lord Mayor's and Sheriffs' Committee (all supporters of the Lord Mayor and Sheriffs) meet on the evening of the Lighting Up Dinner and are summoned to meet the Lighting Up Deputation Sub (Policy and Resources) Committee. This committee is chaired by the Chief Commoner and has five additional members (all Aldermen or Common Councilmen) whose names are determined by ballot. It only meets once and the writer was privileged to be nominated in 2018 to join the Deputation. It should be clear that the Chief Commoner is in charge of the Guildhall and his (or her) permission is needed to use the Guildhall on all occasions. Thus the Lord Mayor's and Sheriffs' Committee appear before this

*A cartoon of the Accident on Lord Mayor's Day published by John Fairburn 1827
from a collection of the London Metropolitan Archives*

Deputation to ask permission to use the Great Hall on November 12th for the Lord Mayor's Banquet (a mere two weeks' hence).

The Deputation quiz the Lord Mayor's and Sheriffs' committee as to their plans and readiness - how many will be attending and how sustainable is the food? Once satisfied, the Chief Commoner announces that permission will be given and in response the Deputation are invited to the Lighting Up Dinner that very evening. Thankfully the Deputation had dressed in black tie in the hope that a dinner would be in the offing.

The Lord Mayor Elect and Sheriffs then arrive and after some refreshment and photographs all move to the Great Hall in order to test the sound system and lighting. Members of the Household Cavalry are present who practise the fanfares to be played at the Banquet and the microphones are tested to adjust to the voices of those making speeches. Finally all move to the crypts for a reception prior to the Lighting Up Dinner.

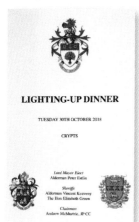

Lighting up dinner menu 2018

The food and wine, an exact copy of that to be eaten at the Banquet, is served to about 90 people. When I attended it consisted of wild mushroom tartlet, coronet of sole and smoked salmon mousseline, highland venison tournedos rossini and lemon posset. There followed the usual toasts with short speeches. The Lord Mayor Elect spoke followed by each of the Sheriffs - who this year spoke as a double act with thanks and humour. At the Banquet the Sheriffs do not speak and so this is their chance to thank their supporters and those present for their help and assistance. Post-dinner drinks are served and a general feeling that the actual Banquet evening will go well was agreed by the guests and hosts alike. The Deputation's job is done but the Committee members are now geared up ready to host the Banquet where they will act as an honour guard escorting the late Lord Mayor, the Prime Minister and other senior guests into the Banquet reception and finally to bid the Lord Mayor goodnight at the very end of the real start to his Mayoral duties.

First published December 2015

You may have noticed that during the recent visit of the President of China, the President attended a Banquet at the Guildhall. It has been a custom for many decades that a visiting Head of State attends a banquet given by the Queen on the first evening and on the next evening is entertained at Guildhall by the Lord Mayor.

Banquet for the President of China in Guildhall attended by HRH Prince Andrew on behalf of the Queen

In the lead up to such occasions much liaison takes place between the City, the Foreign and Commonwealth Office and the Palace. From the City's point of view this is the role of the Remembrancer and his staff. Once the date is agreed the City's well-honed machinery kicks into action. The Court of Common Council vote the cost and nominate a Reception Committee who will be responsible for the arrangements. The members are Aldermen and Common Councilmen, determined in rotation so that every member will have a turn at this role every two to three years. When the Committee meet they elect a Chairman (a hotly contested role) and a Reference Subcommittee. Although most of the work is carried out by the officers (who are very experienced), the Chairmen and Subcommittee determine the caterer, the design of the menu card and the food and wine and have input to all other matters save where protocol prevails.

Caterers are asked to tender for the event and the Reference Subcommittee will make the final choice from their presentations. A tasting is arranged and the Reference Sub will ensure that the correct food and wine is chosen. This is not an easy task. The small group sit down to a tasting comprising a choice of wines from sparkling to port and dessert wines (usually all blind-tasted) while sampling the selection of three separate dinner menus - that is three times four courses. How much each eats (they are fully plated) or drinks is a matter of personal choice. At the end they need to make a decision. There is

Line up of the Lord Mayor Alderman Sir Alan Yarrow and the President of China and HRH Prince Andrew at the Chinese State Banquet

an emphasis on English food and seasonal items but sometimes with a hint of a reference to the country of the visiting Head of State.

Lord Mayor Alderman Sir Andrew Parmley and the King and Queen of Spain

What seems delicious at first bite needs to be tested against a choice of wines and then blended into a four-course meal that looks and tastes as a whole. (It's worth remembering how awful the Queen thought the meal for her 80th birthday lunch was, which had been the choice of the Great British Menu vote of the public.)

The guest list is largely determined by the Palace, FCO and Embassy of the visiting Head of State. All Aldermen and Common Councilmen are invited plus one guest together with the City's High Officers. Being in the Guildhall (which holds up to 700) there is a long list. Guests usually consist of business contacts working in the UK or long-standing expats as well as the party travelling with the Head of State. On the day of the event a seating plan is sent to members to prepare for the conversation that evening - not to seek to change at the last minute. Such plans are often very tricky because of the requirements of seniority and the blend of cultures and businesses.

The menu card is an elaborate document with both menu and toasts but also details of the music to be played (another nod to the visiting country) and some further information and beautiful photos of the country of the visiting Head of State. This is another triumph for the City's diplomacy and becomes a collector's item.

The City traditionally makes a formal address of welcome to the Head of State. This is agreed at Common Council and on the evening is read out at the start of the meal by the Recorder of London and then presented as a beautiful manuscript document in a silver casket specially created and usually flanked with silver City dragons.

On the evening, the Head of State is greeted in Guildhall Yard with an inspection of a military regiment and is met by the Lord Mayor and Lady Mayoress. A representative of the Queen usually attends and for the China Banquet this was Prince Andrew. The other guests have a drinks reception while the VIPs meet in the Art Gallery for drinks, photos and to sign the visitors' book. A small selection of the Senior Aldermen assist the Lord Mayor in hosting these VIP guests.

Drawing entitled "Crumbs from the Rich Man's Table: Distributing food to the Poor at Guildhall after the Lord Mayor's Banquet " by Adrian Marie in the collection of the London Metropolitan Archives 1883

When the guests are seated in the Great Hall the arrival of the Lord Mayor is announced by four State Trumpeters in their gold coats with drum accompaniment at one end of Great Hall and four further State Trumpeters at the other end. The entry music is, of course, the playing of Scipio with a slow hand-clap accompaniment. The procession winds around the tables so everyone can see the guests and officials. The Lord Mayor is preceded at all times by the City Marshal, Sword and Mace.

The meal proceeds and at the end the toasts and speeches are made. There will be a speech by the Lord Mayor of welcome and reference to the links with the City and possibly reference to a visit to the country in question by that Lord Mayor or a predecessor. The Head of State replies and headphones are provided for simultaneous translation. The President of China spoke of his past, growing up in the country and a moment of decision when in reading Shakespeare he had asked himself "To be or not to be". I think we had the answer in his presence at the Banquet.

At the conclusion of the speeches the Lord Mayor, Head of State and senior guests leave Great Hall and others are invited to a stirrup cup in the Old Library. Although the Lord Mayor might return to drink with the guests, the Head of State will leave to return to Buckingham Palace where he or she will be greeted by the Queen and the Duke of Edinburgh who have stayed up to see their safe return.

So who pays? The cost is borne by the City of London Corporation. The City has a fund (City's Cash) that arises from historic investments and gifts to the City (not rate payers or Council Tax money) that is used by the City for such occasions. How much each banquet costs is a matter of speculation as the breakdown of the finances is not public knowledge and so that visiting Heads of State cannot compare the cost of their relative hospitality from the City. A triumph of diplomacy all round.

First published July 2017

E very July the Guildhall is ring-fenced with vehicles large and small, old and new, unique and commonplace and it might feel like a temporary car pound. The line stretches around to Oat Lane (nearly Noble Street) as this is where the horses and carts are thought to feel most at home. It all arises from an historic ceremony performed by the Worshipful Company of Carmen (who use our office space at Plaisterers' Hall). Have you ever attended? It will be held on July 12th in 2017, there is no entry fee, it is a open to all to view a wonderful spectacle and display. I hope to explain why it exists and persuade you to attend this year.

The Worshipful Company of Carmen gained their livery in the reign of Queen Victoria, the only company to do so. It was granted arms in 1929 and received its second royal charter in 1946. But their earlier history is the key to the ancient ceremony of Cart Marking.

Master Carman with the Lord Mayor and others in front of a London double decker bus - all wearing safety gloves presented by the Master Glover, the author

A fellowship of Carmen has existed since 1277 and, as the name suggests, they were hired to carry items in carts or other conveyances around the City. You might be surprised but even then the business was regulated - by the City of London. By the 16th century, cartage was costly, sewage was uncollected and the City needed help. The Carmen obliged. They formed the Fraternyte of Seynt Katryne the Virgyn and Marter of Carters in 1517, and undertook to 'clense, purge and kepe clene' the streets, and carry goods at a reasonable price. They acquired 'carrooms' or stands to ply for hire, effectively licences to trade.

It was not entirely smooth sailing as the Woodmongers (no longer in existence and so you might guess how the story ends) also had carts, and the City granted them licences too. After struggles and changes of fortune the matter was finally resolved. It was agreed that all licensed vehicles should be marked with the City's arms on the shafts and numbered on a brass plate. In 1681 there were 420 licensed carts; in 1835, 600.

The Hallkeeper of the City Corporation (a role that no longer exists) is empowered to licence and mark carrs and carts to stand and ply for hire in the City's streets, so long as the owner is a freeman of the City and a member of the Fellowship of Carmen. Every vehicle has to be brought to Guildhall once a year to be marked. Each year is distinguished by a letter reference, each carr by a number. For the year 2017, the letter will be Z.

In 1899 there were 111 licences in force, held by 16 Carmen; there were also 89 standings or carrooms. As the number of carts declined, the Court of Aldermen reduced the standings. In 1965 the police pointed out that the remaining 18 contravened parking regulations. It was decided to abolish them all except one, which could be specified each year by the Carmen and police. However, cart-marking, it was decided, should continue.

Today, when the new Master and Wardens are installed, normally each October, the Carmen gather outside the appointed City Livery Hall, and one of their number furnishes a carr - sometimes a modern truck, sometimes an older waggon, occasionally horse-drawn - and the Master hires the vehicle before

Master Carman and Master Glover mark a World War I wagon

Master Carman marking City waste collection lorry with enhanced safety features

processing to the church for the Installation Service.

Once a year, in the summer, Carmen bring their horse-drawn waggons and carriages, steamers, veteran and vintage lorries, buses and coaches, and modern trucks and tractor units, to be branded, or marked, with a red-hot iron, on a wooden plate, with the year letter and the carr number, as a reminder of centuries of service to the City and to maintain their ancient tradition. For the Carmen of today are still the carriers of the nation's goods, and the City retains the right of marking.

The Carmen organise the ceremony now in consultation with the City Corporation and the Police. The ceremony starts with the Master Glover presenting the Master Carmen and the Lord Mayor with fire-proof gloves. They are indeed needed as the brands provided by the City Corporation staff are very hot. Each vehicle (which has to be entered by a liveryman of the Carmen) is driven into the Guildhall Yard for the Master's inspection. A wooden licence plate will have been affixed to the vehicle beforehand. The vehicle halts before the dignitaries and the Master Carmen steps forward to "mark" the vehicle using the special brazier and protected by the gloves provided by the Glovers' Company. The Master brands the vehicle with the letter of the year and the Lord Mayor will use a use a different brand with the coat of arms of the City. This is only used on vehicles being marked for the first time. The Master usually shares the duties with the Master Glover. Speaking from experience when I was the Master Glover, the process is not that easy. The brand needs to burn a letter into the wooden licence plate but rather disconcertingly it produces both a flame and then smoke. The first is worrying as you fear for the horses or the petrol tank and then the smoke obscures your actions to create a perfect letter. No second chance allowed.

Once all are marked then the Lord Mayor, Sheriff, Master Carman and Wardens doff their caps as each vehicle passes once again in front of the rostrum on a further parade of all the marked entries. It then seems a shame not to finish the event with an excellent lunch for Carmen and guests in the Great Hall.

This traditional ceremony takes place in the Guildhall Yard where there is plenty of room to watch as well as seeing the vehicles muster in the surrounding streets. A handsome souvenir programme gives guests full details of each entry and proceeds from that and the lunch that follows go towards the Carmen's charity. This year it starts at 11am with the Lord Mayor arriving at about 11:30. The marking finishes with a drive past at about noon and guests leave for lunch around 12:30. There's now no excuse not to know what is going on and why.

First published October 2017

September 28th each year sees the installation of the new Sheriffs of the City of London (following their election at Common Hall by the Livery on June 24th). While the following day (29th) is a very important marker in the Civic year (it is the election of the Lord Mayor at the second Common Hall for the Livery), there is another ancient, but less public ceremony, that relates to the Sheriffs, one I'd like to describe: the Ceremony of the Quit Rents.

Quit Rents ceremony in the Lord Chief Justice's Court

The Ceremony of Quit Rents is the oldest legal ceremony in England, apart from the Coronation, and takes place in early October every year in the Royal Courts of Justice on the Strand in London. This year it will take place on 4th October.

The appointment of the Sheriffs (following election by the Livery) is subject to the approval of the Court of Exchequer (on behalf of the Crown) and payment of a fixed farm rent. The Court of Exchequer was abolished in the mid-19th century when the revenue side of the Court was transferred to the Treasury and to the Chancellor of the Exchequer. The Queen's Remembrancer now takes on the role of the officer of that former Court. For this Quit Rents Ceremony the Court of Exchequer is virtually reconstituted. Its sole purpose is to receive the rents due from the City to the Crown that allow the Sheriffs to serve in office. The ceremony dates back to 1211 and the Queen's Remembrancer is the oldest judicial position in England, created in 1164 by Henry II to keep track of all that was owed to the Crown.

The further curiosity and slightly bizarre element to this event is that the rents are paid for land but no one knows exactly where that land physically is! The amount of rent has not changed over

The horseshoes and nails paid as rent to the Crown

the centuries. The first quit rent due is for land known as 'The Moors', somewhere to the south of Bridgnorth in Shropshire. The earliest record of this dates back to 1211, four years before Magna Carta, when the tenant at the time, one Nicholas de Morrs occupied some 180 acres of land for which he paid rent of two knives, one blunt and one sharp. Over the centuries, the rights of tenancy passed to the City of London. And so traditionally each year the City hands over a blunt billhook (a type of agricultural knife) and a sharp axe to the Queen's Remembrancer.

The second quit rent is for the use of the forge in Tweezer's (or Twizzer's) Alley, somewhere near The Strand. It is believed that the first tenant, Walter Le Brun, was a blacksmith who had set up his business near the tilting ground of the Knights Templar around 1235. Again the tenancy was taken over by the City of London sometime during the intervening centuries. The rent for this land is sixty-one nails and six horse-shoes. The giant horseshoes still used today are said to date back to 1361 and are probably the oldest horseshoes still in existence. They were designed for use in battle or during tournaments where the horses would be trained to lash out with their hooves using the shoes as a weapon to injure their opponents' horses.

The Sheriffs' journey to the ceremony is by boat on the river docking near the Temple and then parading up through the Temple in due ceremony; stopping at Inner Temple to greet the Benchers and then arriving at the Royal Courts of Justice.

The Queen's Remembrancer wears his or her judicial wig under a black tricorn hat, the mark of a judge of the Court of Exchequer. He or she sits at a table covered in a chequered cloth, from which the Court of Exchequer gets its name. In medieval times, the squares on the cloth were used, along with counters, to keep a tally of rents due and rents paid.

During the ceremony the Comptroller and Solicitor of the City presents the horseshoes and nails and counts them out to the Remembrancer who then pronounces "Good number." The knives are tested by taking a hazel stick, one cubit in length, and bending it over the blunt knife and leaving a mark, and the stick is split in two with the sharp knife. This practice stems from the creation of tally sticks where a mark was made in a stick with a blunt knife for each payment counted. When payment was complete the

The Sheriffs and the Queen's Remembrancer

stick was split down the middle, leaving each party with half of the marked stick and creating a receipt (or foil and counter-foil).

The Worshipful Company of Cutlers have the knives made new each year and they bear the hallmark of their Company - the elephant. It must be very galling for them to have to create a blunt knife for this ceremony.

The Ceremony of Quit Rents is open to the public and includes an address by the Queen's Remembrancer often together with a talk on some aspect of London history.

A third quit rent is the subject of a separate ceremony. This rent is due from 1327 for £11 in regard to the reserved interest of the Crown for the 'town of Southwark'. In that year the City was granted its fourth-oldest Royal Charter to acquire Southwark from Edward III for this annual payment. It was specifically retained by Edward VI in the 1550 Charter to the City, which extended its jurisdiction over the outlying parts of Southwark. This quit is rendered by the Foreman of the City's Court Leet Jury of the 'Town and Borough of Southwark', alias Guildable Manor. The ceremony takes place in Southwark at a separate time.

The Queen's Remembrancer also has another very ancient legal duty; the Trial of the Pyx which dates as far back as 1249. Until the 19th century this duty was undertaken at the Court of Exchequer but is now held at Goldsmiths' Hall in the City of London. Every day the Royal Mint collect samples of the coins it produces: this amounts to around 88,000 coins a year. These coins are then placed in boxes (or pyxes) and every February they are brought to Goldsmiths' Hall. The Queen's Remembrancer swears in a jury of 26 goldsmiths whose job it is to count, measure, weigh and assay the coins. In April or May he or she returns to hear the jurors' verdict. The Master Plaisterer is often invited to attend but, thankfully, does not have to count the money.

Coins from the Trial of the Pyx

Prime Warden of the Goldsmiths shows the coinage at the Trial of the Pyx

These ceremonies continue unnoticed and with a great solemnity moderated with a sense of the ridiculous. However I, for one, would never want to see them abandoned.

First published November 2017

Although September 29th each year marks the date that the Lord Mayor is elected at Common Hall by the Aldermen (following the Livery's acclamation of their two preferred candidates), the story does not end there.

The City's right to elect its own Lord Mayor, which is enshrined in the Magna Carta of 1215, also required that the selection by the citizens of London must be ratified by the Monarch. These days the approbation is given by the Lord Chancellor on behalf of the Queen. It was another of the Lord

The Queen's Robing Room in the Palace of Westminster

Chancellor's roles that was not exactly catered for when the office of the Lord Chancellor was set to be abolished. It is now performed by the Minister for Justice - who is the Lord Chancellor!

It takes place in mid-October each year and this year it fell on Monday 16th October. The ceremony takes place in the Palace of Westminster and the Lord Mayor Elect (LME) attends with the Court of Alderman, the City's Chief Officers and select members of his or her family and friends. The Lord Mayor Elect wears his or her violet gown over Court dress (velvet jacket and britches; lace jabot and tights ending in black patent leather shoes with silver buckles). The Alderman wear their violet gowns but over lounge suits and the Sheriffs are in their scarlet gowns.

Such is the importance of the event that the LME is given a blue light police escort from the City to Westminster - he or she travels in one of the large City limousines and the Aldermen and Chief Officers follow in a coach. The resulting parade looks quite unmanageable - except by the City of London Police.

On arrival at the Lords' entrance to the Palace the display of fur, gowns and shapely legs gets some tourists' cameras clicking. But once inside we need to take care and get in order (juniors first) to process to the Queen's Robing Room where the ceremony is held.

The Robing Room is principally used by the Sovereign for the State Opening of Parliament. It is in this room where the Queen puts on the Imperial State Crown and her ceremonial robes before making her way to the House of Lords. While the Aldermen are lined up and waiting we have time to admire the finer features of the room. The fireplace, in front of which the Aldermen stand, was designed by Edward Barry; it is made of marble of different colours from the British Isles and contains two cast-brass statuettes depicting St George fighting the Dragon and St Michael overcoming the Devil. The ceiling of the room is richly panelled and decorated with badges of the monarchs of England.

The paintings in the room by William Dyce depict the

*The City Police blue light escort
to the Palace of Westminster*

chivalric virtues of hospitality, generosity, mercy, religion and courtesy, as represented through scenes from the legend of King Arthur and his court.

There is a lot to take the eye as the Aldermen (who stand throughout) await the arrival of the Lord Chancellor.

The doorkeeper announces "Please rise for the Lord Chancellor" and he or she enters, attired in the finest robe with gold trimmings and is preceded by the purse bearer and the mace bearer appropriately dressed

Exquisite fireplace designed by E M Barry in the Queen's Robing Room

and carrying the insignia of office. The Clerk to the Council is one of the party complete with his or her sword. The Lord Chancellor and party stand in front of the throne as the Aldermen are lined up around the fire place. Bows are exchanged and the family members can return to their seats.

The Recorder of the City of London, in his best attire, including his full bottomed wig, then addresses the Lord Chancellor and informs him of the choice of the citizens to this year's Lord Mayor. The Recorder's speech in 2017 included praise for the Lord Chancellor in his first such ceremony and matters of legal note as well as introducing the LME and recounting his background and family.

Following further bows the Lord Chancellor is handed his speech by the Clerk to the Council and we all wait with bated breath before he confirms: "I am commanded by Her Majesty the Queen to convey Her Majesty's express approval of the choice the Citizens of London in electing you to be Lord Mayor for the coming year…" He too speaks about matters of moment and the suitability of the LME.

At the conclusion of the two speeches the door opens again as two doorkeepers enter, each bearing a loving cup and hand one each to the Lord Chancellor and the LME. The Lord Chancellor raises the cup and toasts My Lord Mayor Elect. The two cups are exchanged and the LME toasts the Lord Chancellor.

The doorkeepers then offer the loving cups to all of the assembled guests starting with the Aldermen and Chief Officers. The cups are followed by trays of warm shortbread. (It is a skill to eat the shortbread and not have crumbs all down one's bear fur trimmed violet gown.)

The Lord Chancellor is introduced to the family of the LME, the Aldermen and the Chief Officers.

At the conclusion of these pleasantries the Lord Chancellor and LME one again bow to each other and then the Lord Chancellor leaves. The LME then departs followed by the Chief Officers and then the Aldermen (seniors first).

The return trip to the City is not so speedy. The police blue light escort cannot be expected simply to get us back to the office and the limousine and coach languish in the traffic on the Embankment.

Only one more hurdle for the LME before he or she can actually take office.

First published February 2015

Every year in January the Lord Mayor hosts a dinner at the Mansion House for the London Governing Bodies. This means an invite to every leader and London Borough Mayor , including the Mayor of London. The Borough Chief Executives attend plus GLA members and various heads of London wide organisations including Transport for London, the Metropolitan Police and London Fire Brigade. This year the Lord Mayor especially invited young students from the City-sponsored Academies so as to bring younger representatives to the dinner. All members of the Common Council and Aldermen attend and it is fair to say that it is a welcome New Year treat, being for many the first collective event of 2015.

Lord Mayor Alderman Sir Alan Yarrow with Mayor Boris Johnson and young student guests

The City have always viewed this as an important platform for the Lord Mayor to speak to these London representatives about the City and his or her view of where London is. The Lord Mayor previewed this dinner in his regular Monday column in City AM. "London faces some crucial challenges in 2015" he said "...the capital's population had reached an all-time high of 8.6 million and would rise even higher in the future ... now is the time for London's representatives to come together and pursue the changes that the capital needs if it is to remain as successful in the future as it has been in the past." The elected members attending were given a top-line briefing on issues that the City wanted to mention to the audience (another exercise of the City's soft power). These included devolution (for London?), Europe, aviation, 'offices to homes' planning policy, air quality, employability and skills, cycle superhighways and policing. (I wonder if these would be in your top eight if you had to prioritise the City's issues as a local authority and global powerhouse?)

Dress code is black tie and there is a delightful array of variations and Mayoral chains and badges in abundance. This is one of the few (maybe the only?) events in the City where the Lord Mayor and the Mayor share the platform. The Egyptian Hall is packed and a fair number of journalists and TV crews attend, too. The Lord Mayor was the first to speak and was keen to stress the unity and strength in all the organisations working together. This year marks various anniversaries but the relevant one for this audience was that it was 50 years since the formation of the London Boroughs in their current configuration. The Lord Mayor mentioned a recent London First report that he applauded for highlighting the need for London to remain "open for business". The Lord Mayor said that London's best chance of success was in all working together. "In 2014, the number of businesses in London shot up by 11%. And almost a third of Britain's new businesses started right here." He described his job as to "sell London" and ended by saying what a good product he had to sell. His toast was "The Mayor of London and the London Assembly, the Court of Common Council, the London Boroughs and the other governing bodies of Greater London."

Next to speak was Jules Pipe, the Mayor of Hackney. He is also the Chairman of London Councils, which is a cross-London organisation of the 32 London Boroughs and the City of London (NB the City of London is not a Borough but is a Corporation which exercises the powers of a local authority!) Jules

complimented the City on the glamorous night in the Mansion House. He emphasised the focus this year with the coming general election and the uncertainty that this would bring until the new Government's budgets were set. A real challenge for the boroughs and the City was how to best secure future services in an era of reduced funding. He posited that devolution was vital because of the need for public service reform, which would be facilitated by such further

Lord Mayor Alderman Peter Estlin with Mayor of London Sadiq Khan

freedom for London.

The last speaker was the Mayor of London, Boris Johnson. He reminded the audience of the fact that any day now a baby would be born who would tip the population over 8.6 million - the highest it had been since 1939. He encouraged the building of more homes - in 1939 there were 2.2 million homes and now there were 3.3 million housing the same number of people. Even so, more homes were needed. He said that London and other cities would benefit from fiscal devolution and a move for more taxes to be kept by cities for them to determine how to spend. Jobs in London would help other cities as well since growth in the capital spreads out to jobs in the rest of the UK.

Mayor of London Sadiq Khan speaking at the Mansion House dinner

The Mayor touched on a tricky and more political issue to do with foreign investment in the capital. "I do not in any way want to deter international investment in our city. Quite the reverse: I want to encourage it. You can see astonishing transformations taking place in London thanks to international investment. We would be utterly nuts as a society if we did anything to turn that away."

The Mayor went on to outline the number of improvements to come to fruition in the next few years - 24-hour tubes, the cycle superhighway etc. The Mayor believed that anyone born today could look forward with happiness that they had been born in the right place at the right time. The audience - Londoners to the core, heartily agreed.

First published June 2015

The Master and several other members of the Livery were fortunate enough to be present at the recent commemoration of Waterloo200. The commemoration of an anniversary such as this is part of the City's role on behalf of the nation and this aspect of the City's role and the City's links with Waterloo are another useful vignette of how the City works.

The City and, frequently, the Lord Mayor have led the nation in celebrating and commemorating

Memorial to the Duke of Wellington in Guildhall by John Bell R.A.

a national event. The close links with St Paul's Cathedral as a focus for the UK at times of celebration and commiseration is an important element on such occasions. A few months ago the end of hostilities in Afghanistan was similarly marked by a service at St Paul's which was followed by a march through the City of the veterans (loudly applauded by many City workers) ending in a reception in Guildhall. On July 7th a service at St Paul's and reception will be held to mark the 10th anniversary of the 7/7 bombings.

Once the decision is made by the Court of Common Council to mark an occasion, the ceremonial work at the Guildhall is choreographed by the Remembrancer's office. Such an event will usually begin with a service at St Paul's. The Lord Mayor will attend in State and greet the members of the Royal family in attendance. The Aldermen and Common Council members attend in their respective scarlet and blue formal robes. They are all seated in the Choir. After the service the Aldermen and Common Councilmen are ferried quickly back to Guildhall (via a fire exit door) in order to be there promptly to greet the guests. Each elected member is allocated a different reception room in the Guildhall so as to provide the widest hospitality and welcome to all the guests.

You might ask why Waterloo was honoured with this level of event? So important was it as a battle at the time that we named a mainline station after it (although we also named Maida Vale after another battle against Napoleon). France, in turn, named one of theirs, Gare d'Austerlitz, after an earlier victory of Napoleon. The battle of Waterloo in 1815 was a major public event at the time and since then there has also been a concerted drive to remember the circumstances of the battle, the defeat of Napoleon and the courage of the combatants in the context of our modern army. Waterloo200 is the charity charged with this task. It is well known to the Plaisterers, as the charity has been using our offices in Plaisterers' Hall for planning over the last year or so. The charity was requested by the UK Government to create a long-lasting educational legacy stemming from the bicentenary events of 2015. This programme is

Frieze of the battle of Waterloo at the base of the memorial in Guildhall

focused on encouraging schools from across the country to engage with the story of the battle. The charity has also been promoting all bicentenary events and exhibitions across Europe of which this one held in the City is most prominent.

The links with the City are, however, equally as fascinating. Between 1811 and 1813 the Court of Common Council passed several resolutions of thanks to the Duke of Wellington, Commander of the Allied Armies. The City honoured the Duke in several ways. On May 9th 1811 he was awarded the Honorary Freedom of the City of London with a Sword of the value of 200 guineas. On September 23rd 1812, following his victory at Salamanca, Common Council passed a resolution of thanks to Wellington and added a gold box to the Freedom of the City already accorded to him. Following victories over the French near Vittoria another resolution was passed by Common Council, 12 July 1813. Following the Treaty

of Paris in May 1814, Wellington was entertained at the Guildhall on July 9th 1814 and the opportunity was taken of actually presenting him with the Freedom of the City, which he had hitherto been unable to take up (presumably too busy away from London on campaigns), and also with the Sword of Honour and gold box. This dinner is itself the subject of a painting now in the Guildhall Art Gallery showing the sumptuous affair that it was. In 1814 Napoleon had been defeated and in exile and the Treaty of Paris had been signed creating peace in Europe. Swords of honour were voted by the City to the commanders in chief of the other armies and presented at the Banquet. The Emperor of Russia and King of Prussia attended as did the Prince

Statue of the Duke of Wellington outside the Royal Exchange

Banquet to celebrate the Duke of Wellington in Guildhall 1814

Regent. Such was both the scale and splendour of City entertaining in that day and age. The sword presented to Field Marshall Blucher is held by the Museum of London and soon to be exhibited in the Chamberlain's Court with various other important memorabilia relating to Wellington.

Following the great victory at Waterloo, the City passed another resolution of thanks "For the consummate ability, unexampled exertion and irresistible ardour displayed by him on the June 18th on which day the decisive victory over the enemy was obtained". This illuminated Resolution is currently on display in the City's Heritage Gallery (down the stairs at the Art Gallery entrance to Guildhall). It will be on display until October 1st 2015 and so members attending the election of the Lord Mayor on September 29th will be able to see this. The Common Council also resolved "that a bust of his Lordship be placed in the Common Council Room of this City, in order that the Citizens of London... may ever have recalled to their recollection the glorious deeds of the great military hero of their country...".

A further statue, by John Bell, was erected in 1857 and was illuminated in Guildhall especially for the reception and mentioned by the Lord Mayor in his speech of welcome on June 18th 2015. Since Wellington passed half his life in peace and half in war the statue is intended to reflect this balance in his life. Peace is seated at the Duke's right hand and extends a civic wreath looking up gratefully towards him. War is on his left leaning on a sheathed sword and grasping a victor's wreath - resting from his labours. The Duke rests his left hand on his field-marshal's baton and holds the Peace of 1815 in his right. The main panel beneath the Duke shows the last charge at Waterloo. It is certainly worth viewing when next in Guildhall. A footnote in the City's archives shows that in the bombing in 1940 the Duke's baton and the hand of Peace were both damaged - but both have been replaced satisfactorily to the untrained eye. The statue is situated immediately opposite the centre of the Guildhall where the Lord Mayor will be seated with the main guests at any of his banquets. One can only imagine the comments made behind the scenes regarding the seating before the State Banquet to President Sarkozy of France.

If it is not too crass to mention, the City funds the cost of such events from its fund called City's Cash. Guests will, I hope, attest that it was most enjoyable but it certainly did not match the lavishness of the 1814 banquet. However, the warmth of welcome and finesse of the arrangements means that the prestige of the day and the efforts of Waterloo200 will resonate far and wide.

First published September 2012

The Guildhall is the location for many City events and all liverymen have at least two opportunities each year to attend Common Hall, which is held in Great Hall, Guildhall. But when you next attend Common Hall and wait patiently for the proceedings to commence you might like to dwell upon some of the history, usage and current purposes of the Guildhall complex. The current building was substantially built in 1411 although it did replace a previous building on this site. That earlier and smaller building was itself within the footprint of the Roman amphitheatre - but my intention with this article is to bring matters up to date rather than to bury them further in the ancient past!

The Dance Porch added to the medieval Guildhall in 1788

By the end of the 14th century London's merchants were developing civic administration along with their ambitions. While King Richard II had completed his re-modelling of Westminster Hall, Londoners were anxious to match, if not surpass, that achievement. They turned to John Croxtone, an unsung hero of the City. His plan was to raise the Great Hall on a double crypt. The western crypt formed part of the old Guildhall and a new western crypt. Croxtone's design is still visible and largely extant. The original roof was destroyed in the Great Fire and Wren's refurbishment was itself replaced by a 19th-century roof which then suffered from the Blitz on 29 September 1940. Giles Gilbert Scott was given the task of refurbishment and reverted to the original Croxtone design with some additional windows. So the Guildhall is very truly medieval.

The original building took some 20 years to create; however, Croxtone had to petition on several occasions to receive his payment and accommodation and this is despite his work not only on the

The interior of the medieval Great Hall

Guildhall but also on a new Leadenhall Market and the great Cheapside Cross.

Space was in short supply even in these early days and so much of the exterior of Great Hall was crowded in by a chapel, library and court rooms for the Aldermen. Much of this has since been removed and more can be seen of the 15th-century building than would have been visible to Croxtone's contemporaries. Within the mix of medieval City characters one must not overlook the role of Richard Whittington whose death and consequential beneficence to the City allowed some of the money from the Whittington estate to pave and glaze the new Guildhall and to pay for the new stone building to the east of the Guildhall Yard which was to be the start of the City's library. Needless to say this was an immensely expensive project. It was paid for by an early public/private funding arrangement. For 10 years the City doubled the fees charged for enrolling apprentices and the purchasing of freedom as well as the fines for transgressions such as selling food underweight. Even after the first 10-year period the fees were still used for work on the Guildhall. Many private individuals were happy to contribute to the project and specified in their wills that money was to go to "Novo Operi Guyhalde Civitatis".

The next major development was by George Dance who in 1788 designed the now famous gothic-style porch that forms the backdrop to so many photographs of the election of the Lord Mayor. But in the 20th century a rash of new building has been undertaken. We have seen the addition of the north block (designed by Giles Gilbert Scott) in the mid-1950s and refurbished in 2009. This now houses meeting rooms, offices and the important Chamberlain's Court where the Freedom of the City is dispensed. The west wing was added in the mid-1970s in a modernist style by Giles' son Richard Gilbert Scott. Again liverymen will visit this to use the various meeting rooms that are available free to livery companies for meetings as well as the Guildhall Club and private dining room.

The top floor has some basic overnight accommodation that is available for the members of Common Council and occasional use by Livery Masters. Guildhall Yard east is now the location of the Guildhall Art Gallery

The State Banquet to the King and Queen of Spain with Great Hall dressed to impress

The Roman Amphitheatre below the Guildhall Art Gallery

Guildhall Yard showing the dark slate line of stones marking the extent of the Amphitheatre below the Yard and The Guildhall Art Gallery

and associated meeting rooms including the City Marketing Suite that houses the scale model of the City of London. Building plans commenced here after the previous site was bombed in the Second World War but lack of funds, general delay and the unexpected discovery of the Roman amphitheatre in 1988 meant that the building was only reopened in 1999. This, too, was designed by son Richard in a post-modernist style. The bulk of the premises are occupied by the offices of the City of London Corporation. A rationalisation of the City's own premises in 2009 meant that the majority of the staff are based in Guildhall - the Town Clerk's department, Finance, Planning, Surveyor's, Legal, Social Services and Economic Development. Only what has to be external (Cleansing, Cemeteries, Port Health Authority and Open Spaces) are off site and close to the services that they deliver.

Returning to Great Hall, this has been used as a meeting place for livery companies over many centuries. The Court of Common Council meets here approximately every

The Dance Porch lit up with the flag of St George for Lumiere Celebration

six weeks on a Thursday lunchtime. Meetings are open to the public and details are available of meeting dates on the City of London website (www.cityoflondon.gov.uk). Copies of the agenda and public reports are available on the website approximately seven days before the meeting. Outside of formal City meetings Great Hall is used for many public events. Famous external uses include the annual award of the Man Booker Prize. However, perhaps, the event covered with the most widespread TV coverage is the Lord Mayor's Banquet, which takes place on the Monday immediately following the Lord Mayor's Show. At this event speeches are given not only by the new and the late Lord Mayor but also by the Prime Minister, Lord Chancellor and Archbishop of Canterbury.

The walls of Great Hall must resound with many famous scenes from the trial of Lady Jane Grey who was taken from Great Hall and beheaded at the Tower to the speech of our Queen in her "annus horribilis".

A visit, whether you are surrounded by fellow liveryman, an excited diner or dropping in alone, will always be well rewarded.

First published November 2014

The City of London hosts over 200 open spaces within the square mile. In total these spaces amount to just over 32 hectares. Unbelievable? Well we host one ourselves at Plaisterers' Hall. The garden outside the hall running the length of Noble Street is also the site of one of the largest remaining sections of the Roman Wall. Following the completion of Plaisterers' Hall in the early 1970s, the Company turned its attention to the interesting but then, rather un-prepossessing bomb site outside. So it was that to commemorate Her Majesty the Queen's Silver Jubilee in 1977 that the Plaisterers' approached the City Corporation with the suggestion that the Plaisterers might clear all the accumulated rubbish away, expose the foundations of the Roman Wall and establish a natural garden. Not surprisingly the City readily agreed and for the past 36 years we have been paying our dues like good citizens, being one Jubilee Crown. We

Surveying the Plaisterers' gardens

ensure that the garden is well kept. But it is no ordinary garden as it is intended to preserve species with minimal intervention. Although in part mowed grass, the southern end is left to grow (seemingly unkempt) and that area is only mown once a year. Between May and July this year a plant survey was carried out and the following has been recorded.

"The garden was reseeded about 10 years ago but since then has been left to develop its current species-rich flora with minimal intervention of annual mowing. It is not open to the public so remains undisturbed but can be viewed from above. The Friends of the City Gardens (who carried out the survey) found over one hundred species were identified, including rarities such as black mulberry and upright vetch as well as more common meadow species such as Field Scabious, Yellow Rattle, Black Medick, Greater Knapweed and many more. The walls are home to Red Valerian, Purple Toadflax and Long headed Poppy. All of the data will be entered on the Green Space Information for Greater London (GiGL) database."

This useful and scientific review has

St Dunstan's in the West gardens

The gardens at Plaisterers' Hall

led in turn to our Plaisterers' garden being entered into the City in Bloom competition. This competition mirrors the national campaigns with similar names but the scope and scale of entries and spaces to judge is tremendous. It includes gardens, parks, window boxes and green roofs. The Plaisterers' Garden had been shortlisted and at the award ceremony on October 27th we did not win a prize, but Lee White (Assistant Facilities Manager) got a special mention for the beautiful wild flower garden at Plaisterers' Hall .

The City has been careful to preserve these green spaces. The City of London website (www.cityoflondon.gov.uk) provides details of all these spaces and the scheme across the City. They are maintained by the City gardeners, by businesses and by individuals. The Friends of City Gardens, a group of volunteers who love the green spaces, work closely with the City of London Corporation's Gardens team to help make these gardens greener and more accessible for everyone. Many have been preserved since they were churchyards and are near existing or former churches. St Dunstan in the East is a favourite of mine just off Eastcheap. I most remember it as the spot where I sat for an anxious half an hour before my interview for my first job as an Articled Clerk.

Other spaces come into being as a result of planning conditions on new developments where the City planners see the need to create spaces for people to sit and reflect (although many get overrun with smokers and the attendant butt bins). See Angel Lane that adjoins the Nomura building on Upper Thames Street running down to the Thames. The Barbican gardens are included in the English Heritage Register of Gardens of Special Interest and in part open to the public. They include the Barbican Conservatory, which is open most Sundays (but do check for exact times).

Some of the gardens are actually for playing in. At St Botolph's Without Bishopgate gardens there is a tennis and netball court open all year and other children's play areas are at Tower Hill Gardens, West Smithfield Rotunda Garden, Portsoken Street and St Peter's Hill Walkway. There are organised garden walks during the summer and information is available from the City of London Information Centre. There is also a self-guided tree trail.

Today the greenery extends in the City of London to over 70,000 square metres of green roofs. These

The rooftop garden over Cannon Street station

vary from intensively planted roof terraces to extensive green roofs that may be sedum mats or wild flower meadows with areas of bare pebbles. These rooftop areas are important new habitats for wildlife in the City and have enhanced the diversity of the City's bird life as well as supporting many bee colonies. They are not so visible or accessible but if you ever get a chance to go up high you can see some greener and pleasanter views over the rooftops and terraces of the City.

A new way of visiting the City Gardens is provided in an audio-tour by City Gardener Nicholas Martin. His tour of Postman's Park is fun to hear. This scenic park acquired its name due to its popularity as a lunchtime garden with workers from the nearby old General Post Office. It is home to the famous Watts memorial, built in 1900 by Victorian painter and philanthropist GF Watts (1817-1904). This memorial is a really unique homage to everyday heroes and heroines of London.

There is always more to explore in the rich and diverse City of London

First published April 2015

We are lucky to have in the City of London and close to our wonderful Hall, some beautiful churches that are not well known to all Plaisterers. They are under the stewardship of Alan McCormack who is the engaging Rector at St Vedast-alias-Foster. His warm welcome will be remembered by members of the Livery who have attended our Christmas Carol Services in recent years at St Vedast. I have been to see Alan to find out more about his life and background and the Churches within his benefice.

Revd. Dr Alan McCormack

Alan hails from Northern Ireland where he went to school and grew up. He was ordained in 1996 at the time of the referendum on the Good Friday Agreement, which to his delight was approved by a majority of both Protestants and Roman Catholics. Alan attended Jesus College, Oxford and read Theology with a special focus on Hebrew. He then read for a DPhil in Classical Hebrew poetics at Oxford. Alan's first ministry, where he served title, was in East Belfast. He then became Dean and Chaplain of Trinity College, Dublin for nine years.

St Vedast - Alias - Foster

It was from there that Alan was recruited for his present position in London by Bishop Richard Chartres, the current Bishop of London. Alan quickly settled into London life and has made many friends. He enjoys music, cooking and martial arts (so do not cross him!). His friendly manner and his obvious interest in people, coupled with his quick wit, makes him very interesting company.

Alan lives next door to St Vedast-alias-Foster where he is the Rector. St Vedast is a beautiful Wren church. It is one of only a few city churches open seven days a week. There is a church hall and courtyard. The courtyard is rather hidden and usually very peaceful (although not so on St Patrick's Day!) The church hall is used by numerous community groups and is popular for children's parties (www.vedast.org.uk). The church has links with a number of Livery Companies including the Plaisterers. Indeed the site of our three original halls was within the St Vedast's parish, near Wood Street. St Vedast is linked to The Church of the Incarnation on Madison Avenue in New York and there are regular exchanges and interaction to keep the two churches in contact sharing ideas and people.

St Vedast's sister church is St Botolph without Bishopsgate. St Botolph's is a large active church serving the eastern side of the City. Alan is the Rector here, also. Two major services are held weekly, on Wednesday and Thursday lunchtimes and the church has an active musical tradition. It is set in a large garden with a hall and courts for tennis and netball. St Botolph's is of medieval origin. It survived the Great Fire but fell into disrepair, it was rebuilt in 1788-91. St Botolph was a seventh-century East Anglian saint. The church underwent several restorations during the 19th and 20th centuries. The plain exterior is in contrast to what John Betjeman called an "exalting" succession of features inside.

The interior has wooden galleries, a highly decorated plaster work ceiling and, at the east end, the only 18th-century stained glass window in the City of London, a depiction of the Agony in the Garden. Some of the stained glass is Victorian and some monuments were preserved from the old church.

I now turn to a church in Gresham Street: St Anne and St Agnes. The first mention of a church on the site is in documents of 1137, which refer to St Agnes near Alderychgate. The church was gutted by fire in 1548, rebuilt and then destroyed in the Great Fire of London in 1666. It was rebuilt by Sir Christopher Wren in 1680 and extensively restored in the 18th and 19th centuries. Unfortunately on December 30th 1940 it was again destroyed, this time by German bombing. It was rededicated in 1966 largely through donations by the Worldwide Lutheran Church. The building is now called the Gresham Centre and has become the home of Voces Cantabiles Music, an educational project of the vocal ensemble Voces 8. Past parishioners have included John Milton, John Bunyan and John Wesley (a relative of Susanne's) who preached at the church in 1758.

I finally mention All Hallows Church-on-the-Wall, London Wall. It is adjacent to the former city wall at Broad Street. It was constructed in 1767 replacing an earlier church built some time in the early 12th century on a bastion of the old Roman Wall. The earlier church became renowned for its hermits who lived in cells in the church. Like St Botolph's, All Hallows escaped destruction in the Great Fire due to its position under the wall but subsequently fell into dereliction. In 1767 the architect George Dance the Younger rebuilt the church after returning from Italy where he studied classical buildings. The new All Hallows took its inspiration from the classical world and was remarkably simple in form, with no aisles, its interior consists solely of a barrel-vaulted nave with a half dome apse at the far end and decoration deriving from the Ancient Temple of Venus and Rome in the Italian capital. All Hallows was damaged in the Second World War and restored in the 1960s. It is the church of the Worshipful Company of Carpenters. It is now the home of the urban youth

St Botolph without Bishopsgate

charity XLP and City Gates Church, a congregation with roots in the British New Church Movement.

In addition to his duties in the churches that I have mentioned Alan is also involved in the development of a new church in Tottenham Hale - here (the first new Church of England Church to be built in London for 40 years) he is resourcing financially and pastorally the work of The Revd. Andrew Williams as Priest Missioner. This is a project to create Christian worship in a new development in a less affluent part of London. Alan finds his work there very rewarding.

I hope this article has been of interest to Liverymen and I am ready to arrange an opportunity for any Plaisterer who would like to visit any of the churches mentioned in this article. We are indeed fortunate to have some lovely historical churches near our Hall and a Rector in Alan McCormack who cares for them and their parishioners.

Past Master Richard Hanney

The Rector of St Vedast in 2019 is Rev. Paul Kennedy

First published May 2017

You may have noticed lots of elevated walkways or bridges spanning many of the City of London roads. Indeed, you may have used them to ease your crossing. That adjacent to the Hall stretches across London Wall from One London Wall to the highwalk that easily leads you to the Museum of London if you turn left or El Vinos if you turn right - depending on your taste.

High walk greening on Pedway at St Alphage Highwalk

The arrangement of these walkways is in fact called the City of London Pedway Scheme. It is a partial elevated pedway that evolved out of a plan to transform traffic flows in the City of London by separating pedestrians from street level traffic using elevated walkways. First devised as part of the post-Second World War reconstruction plans for London, it was put into effect mainly from the mid-1950s to the mid-1960s and eventually abandoned by the 1980s - until now.

Versions of the plan had been under consideration since the 19th century, and given shape by the German Bauhaus movement, but the scheme was only given impetus in London after the Second World War, during which London had suffered severe bomb damage. Enthusiasts for the scheme saw an opportunity to put it into practice through the post-war reconstruction programme, and in 1947 architect Charles Holden and planner William Holford developed a blueprint that envisaged a network of first-floor walkways that would connect buildings across the City.

By the mid-1960s, the City of London Corporation had incorporated the scheme into its development plan. Although no coherent network was ever defined, designers of new developments were required to incorporate first-floor access to the pedway network as a condition of being granted planning consent. As most of the network had not been built, this meant that many developments incorporated unused "dead space" at first-floor level and partial walkways that led to dead ends. In consequence, the scheme was unpopular with many architects.

The plan had the backing of city planner Percy Johnson-Marshall who compared the scheme to Venice; the city streets were like canals and the pedway the bridges over them. In reality it meant offices had two sets of receptions, one at street and one at pedway level (ever tried to get into 125 London Wall?). Shops built at pedway level found it difficult to get deliveries, shops at street level had no customers. Poor design meant the pedways were windswept and prone to flooding. People feared the pedways' lack of use would lead to a cycle of decline.

Buildings that were required to incorporate links to the pedway included in their heyday the National Westminster Tower, which incorporated a pedestrian bridge across Bishopsgate that was never used and is now demolished; the Commercial Union building, the Barbican, and Drapers' Gardens.

By the mid-1980s, the scheme had effectively been discontinued. The reason for its ultimate demise were escalating costs and the increase in influence of the conservation lobby, which opposed the extensive redevelopment of the historic areas of the City. Not to mention concerns about security due to the additional access points.

The pedway scheme only succeeded in establishing itself in areas that required extensive post-war reconstruction. The most extensive part of the network to be completed was in the Barbican Estate

New Pedways running parallel to London Wall

and surrounding streets. Indeed the clue to getting around the Barbican is to access all areas via the highwalks. The main entrance to the Museum of London is, to this day, at first-floor level. Indeed this is rather a disadvantage to the Museum as many people claim not be able to find the entrance - even though there are six well-signposted points at ground floor level leading up to the highwalk by stairs, escalators and lifts. The new Museum of London site at Smithfield will be at ground floor level and will be much more accessible - maybe somewhat of a reaction to the current high level isolation.

Pedways have now returned in style with the new development known as London Wall Place. This large new office development is a few hundred yards from the Hall towards Moorgate. The development threatened to cut off the Barbican residents from their previous high-level traverse to the City and thus the planning conditions imposed required the developer to reinstate and improve the pedways. These weathered-steel beauties are the first additions to the pedway network in many years. True, they are a replacement for a demolished walkway rather than an entirely new piece of infrastructure. But their attractive, sinuous form is a far cry from the utilitarian concrete spans they replaced.

A film was made about the network in 2013 called The Pedway: Elevating London *https://vimeo.com/80787092*, which describes this interesting piece of architecture's place in the post-war redevelopment in the City of London. Featuring interviews with professor of town planning Michael Hebbert (UCL), architecture critic Jonathan Glancey, former City planning officer Peter Wynne Rees and writer Nicholas Rudd-Jones (Pathways), the film explores why the pedway scheme was unsuccessful and captures the abandoned remains that, unknown to the public, still haunt the square mile. It's worth watching and then setting out on foot to find the lost stairways.

The gentle destruction of the pedways has driven pedestrians to the pavements and the consequential conflict with traffic. The resolution to that conundrum is more traffic-free and traffic-light areas and wider pavements. A future 'Bank on Safety' scheme is planned at the busy Bank junction, and more changes will occur with the Barbican Ultra Low Emission Zone and Cultural Hub. All of which are planned to make the City more liveable.

One wonders how they will be viewed in 50 years' time - will they, like pedways, have given way to better architectural innovations?

First published December 2017

"So long as the Stone of Brutus is safe, so long will London flourish"

The Museum of London is just across the road from Plaisterers' Hall and worth a visit at any time. It is a treasure trove of London's history. But the particular focus of this article is to consider the London Stone that is temporarily housed there while building work is taking place.

The London Stone is an object of wonder and myth and was originally located in Dowgate ward (where

The London Stone newly positioned in Cannon Street

The unveiling of the London Stone by Lord Mayor Alderman Charles Bowman and the Master Mason

I am the elected City of London Alderman). The London Stone has a chequered and long history. It was moved across Cannon Street (formerly Candlewick Street) in the 18th century and is now in Walbrook ward. This has been a point of issue between the two wards ever since. It is currently lodged at the Museum of London (Aldersgate ward) and is being well looked after until the building on Cannon Street (north side) is rebuilt and the London Stone can be returned in all its glory to a prominent and important location in the new building on that site.

Is too much being made of this scheduled ancient monument? It's been claimed to be a Druidic altar, a Roman milestone, and the magical 'heart of London'. It's one of London's most ancient landmarks, but most people have never heard of it - or if they have, they've heard one of the strange legends that have sprung up around it.

The stone itself is oolitic limestone, of a type first brought to London for building and sculptural purposes in the Roman period - but also used in Saxon and medieval times. It originally stood towards the southern edge of the medieval Candlewick Street opposite St Swithin's church (called 'St Swithin at London Stone' by at least 1557). This would have placed it in front of the great Roman building, often identified as the provincial governor's palace, which stood on the site now occupied by Cannon Street Station. It has been suggested that the Stone was originally some sort of monument erected in the palace forecourt. Some have described it - without any evidence - as being a Roman 'milliarium', the central milestone from which distances in the Roman province of Britain were measured.

On the other hand, it also stands at the centre of the grid of new streets laid out after King Alfred re-established London in 886, after Viking attacks had destroyed the original Saxon town, so it may have served some significant function for late Saxon Londoners. And it must be at this period that it received its singular name - Lundene Stane in Old English. The presence of this object gave a name to the area in which it was situated such that our first Mayor of London, Henry Fitz-Ailwyn, was said to be of London Stone (in the same way that our own current Lord Mayor is from Essex!).

John Strype, in his 1720 updated edition of John Stow's Survey of London, seems to have been the first to offer the proposal that London Stone was "an Object, or Monument, of Heathen Worship" erected by the Druids. Thus, later, London Stone was to play an important but not always consistent role in the visionary works of William Blake, prominent among them being its identification as an altar stone upon which Druids carried out bloody sacrifices.

Where Albion slept beneath the Fatal Tree,
And the Druids' golden Knife
Rioted in human gore, In Offerings of Human Life…
They groan'd aloud on London Stone,
They groan'd aloud on Tyburn's Brook…

There is no evidence for this, and London Stone, whatever its purpose, was certainly not erected before the Roman period.

London Stone entered national history briefly in the summer of 1450, when John or Jack Cade, leader of the Kentish rebellion against the corrupt government of Henry VI, entered London and, striking London Stone with his sword, claimed to be 'lord of this city'. There is no recorded precedent for his action, and contemporary chroniclers were at a loss as to its significance. We know the story best from Shakespeare's Henry VI Part Two, in which Cade seats himself on the stone as on a throne, issues proclamations, and passes swift judgement on the first unfortunate man to offend him. It is at this point in the play that there is uttered the well-known words "The first thing we do, let's kill all the lawyers".

The London Stone temporarily housed at the Museum of London for safekeeping

This is great theatre; it is also fiction - but it has led to the belief that London Stone was traditionally used for such purposes. Shakespeare's inventive genius has a lot to answer for.

It seems to have been damaged by the Great Fire of 1666, which destroyed all the surrounding buildings. By 1720 what was left of the stone was protected by a small stone cupola built over it, and in 1742 it was moved as a traffic hazard, to be placed, still within its protective cupola, on the north side of the street against the door of the new Wren church of St Swithin. Two further moves, in 1798 and in the 1820s, placed it eventually where it was to remain for more than 100 years, built into the middle of the church's south wall.

The Wren church was gutted by bombing in the Second World War, but the walls were left standing and London Stone remained in place until 1960, when it was moved to the then Guildhall Museum (at that time housed in the Royal Exchange) for safekeeping. After the demolition of the ruins and the completion of the new building on the site to house the Bank of China, in October 1962 the Stone was placed in the specially constructed grilled and glazed alcove in the wall that it occupied until recently.

The London Stone being guarded by the City Police 1926

By the end of the 18th century romantic writers were beginning to suggest a relationship between the survival of London Stone and the well-being of London itself. This recalled the legendary 'palladium' of Greek mythology, the statue of Pallas Athene that protected the city of Troy. So Thomas Pennant, in a history of London published in the 1790s, commented 'it seems preserved like the Palladium of the city…'.

This concept received a great boost from the apparent discovery of an 'ancient saying': 'So long as the Stone of Brutus is safe, so long will London flourish'. This first appeared in print in an article in the periodical Notes and Queries in 1862 - apparently no previous writer was aware of it. Where did this 'ancient saying' come from, and why had it been forgotten until 1862? And why 'the Stone of Brutus'? The article retails a supposed legend that London Stone was set up by Brutus of Troy, the first king of Britain. This notion is rooted in a much older piece of made-up history: the legend that London was first founded by Brutus, leader of a group of Trojan colonists, as Troia Nova, or New Troy. The article was written (under a pseudonym) by the Revd. Richard Williams Morgan, Anglican priest, Welsh patriot, bard, and later the founder of his own Ancient British Church. For Morgan, the Welsh, who were superior to the English in every way, were directly descended from Brutus and the Trojan immigrants. There can be no doubt that the idea that legendary Brutus brought the Stone from Troy and the saying about London's fate if the Stone is lost or damaged are both his own inventions. Sadly, Morgan's fantasy is still quoted as if it were an authentic medieval proverb.

A modern myth has arisen that the Lord Mayor of London serves as a 'custodian' or 'guardian of the Stone'. It is an obvious concept, but belief in a guardian of London Stone does not seem ever to have existed in historical times, nor does the City of London Corporation list it as one of the Lord Mayor's official duties. In fact, until 1972, when London Stone was officially listed (Grade II*) as a structure of special historic interest, neither the Corporation nor the Lord Mayor seems to have taken any responsibility for the Stone. Ownership of the Stone itself has meanwhile passed with ownership of the land on which it has stood for nearly 300 years, the site of St Swithin's Church.

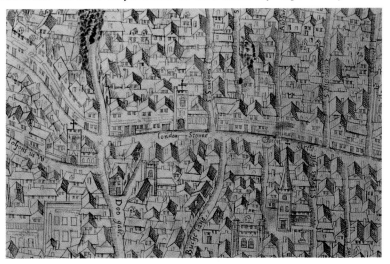

In the late 19th century the folklorist George Laurence Gomme put forward his opinion that London Stone was London's 'fetish stone': He stated: "In early Aryan days, when a village was first established, a stone was set up. To this stone the head man of the village made an offering once a year." The Lord Mayor was therefore the lineal descendant of the first 'village head man' of London.

The London Stone shown on the first copperplate map of London 1558

This authoritative statement by a well-respected folklorist had a great influence on other writers. In 1937 another folklorist, Lewis Spence, published a book on Legendary London, in which he claimed the 'Brutus' legend as a traditional memory of actual historic events. Authors interested in geomancy (the magic of the landscape) have identified the Stone as a 'mark stone' on several leylines. Others fear its removal from its original location has violated the integrity of the City's sacred geometry.

Myth or fact there is an aura about the London Stone. There is something of the beating heart of London about an item that has withstood all the factual and historical vicissitudes listed. Indeed, although the Museum has cared lovingly for the Stone it was only two weeks after the Stone moved to the Museum that the Brexit referendum took place!

With thanks to John Clark former curator at the Museum of London

The London Stone was replaced on the north side of Cannon Street and unveiled in a ceremony by the Lord Mayor on 4th October 2018.

39. THE CITY OF LONDON'S PUBLIC LIBRARIES

First published March 2018

It may come as no surprise to you that the City of London Corporation acting as a local authority is responsible for providing a public library service.

First I should mention the Guildhall Library, which is for reference use only and was built between March 1423 and September 1425 by the executors of Mercer and former Lord Mayor, Richard Whittington and the executors of another Mercer, William Bury. It has been claimed that Guildhall Library was the first 'public' library in England and maybe some citizens were allowed access, but it was primarily for the use of the priests at the college. I want in this article to concentrate on the other public lending libraries of which the City can be justly proud and of which you can become members - whether or not you live in or pay your council tax to the City of London Corporation.

To join a City library you can sign up online or in person at any of the libraries (just bringing a proof of identity and address with you). Membership gives you access to all of the libraries.

The Barbican Library is the closest to Plaisterers' Hall and is the most convenient and accessible for members not living in the City. There is a wide range of services including a dedicated children's and music library, special collections in art, music, finance and London, graphic novels, books and audio books, a home delivery service, CDs, DVDs and language sets, free Wi-Fi and computers with internet access, reading groups and friendly, expert staff.

The Barbican Music Library is housed within the main Barbican Library and has the largest selection of CDs in any London public library together with scores, music books and magazines and listening booths. There are two electronic pianos available for customers to use, free of charge and they provide headphones in exchange for ID. Vocal scores and orchestral sets are for hire and can be sourced but there is a requirement that the regular rehearsal venue for the choir or orchestra using the scores must be within the City of London.

The Barbican Music Library promotes Unsigned London. This is aimed at promoting music by artists without a record deal who are based in the London area by stocking their CDs in the library. Music of all genres is accepted and it is a great and easy way of promoting music and attracting new fans as the public can borrow the CDs for free.

The City of London Library Home Delivery Service will deliver books and more to City of London residents who are unable to get to a library by themselves. This might not apply to you! This could be due to old age, a disability, an inability to carry heavy books or a temporary injury or ailment that restricts someone to their home. The Library will provide a wide range of library materials such as novels, non-fiction, large print, standard print, music CDs, talking books and DVDs.

Artizan Street Library is based in E1 and Shoe Lane Library in EC4. Both provide a wide range of services for busy local residential and business areas. The list of services comprises room hire, books, audio books and daily newspapers, DVDs, CDs and language sets, free Wi-Fi and computers, rhymetime and Stay and Play for under-fives, reading groups and a home delivery service. There are also keep-fit classes, with Zumba and Pilates both offered.

The City's eLibrary is really an extension of the physical library. Members with internet access can access the library remotely, renew library books and avoid fines. They can also access eBooks and eAudio books as well as magazines and other resources all from their home location.

All of the above might be available in your local town or neighbourhood, but there is one further useful library befitting the City of London - the City Business Library (CBL). This is located in the Guildhall. It is a public library dedicated to business information, offering free access to a comprehensive collection of business databases and publications, including general start up advice, market research, company information, statistics and business news. Together with the expert staff on hand this means that a variety of needs are met for the sole trader: start-up; microenterprise; entrepreneur; SME; charity; social enterprise; job-seeker and anyone who needs business information.

Dragon Café at Shoe Lane Library

The CBL runs numerous courses on starting up your own business, marketing and social media, the perfect elevator pitch, starting business overseas and getting a job.

The spur to writing this article now is a new project that the Barbican and Community Libraries are participating in along with many other public libraries round the county. Funded by the Wellcome Trust and Carnegie UK the City libraries are creating a Dragon Café in the City. This new project, based at Shoe Lane Library, is to provide City workers and residents a space to relax and recharge in the Square Mile. Taking place every fortnight until July 2018 there will be a range of wellbeing activities and events. This will help City workers de-stress as well as cope with the problems of mental ill health and anxiety that are ever-present in our busy City.

The activities are open to all and people can just turn up and relax in the sanctuary space of the library: read a book, reflect on the day, have a cup of tea, chat to friends or new acquaintances. The first day included a professional costumier leading a mask workshop looking at identity, what we choose to reveal and conceal about ourselves, and how to work towards personal goals. A chess master gave a fascinating session looking at strategy and game

Children enjoying the City's library space

City Business Library at Guildhall

development, ideally for those with knowledge of the game of chess looking to improve. A terrarium-making workshop taught people how to make their own terrarium to take away. They will also be providing a Games and Craft Station for mindful creativity, drawing, colouring and relaxing board games and jigsaw playing throughout the day and the regular Craft group will be meeting for sewing, knitting, crocheting and chatting!

Loneliness is another major public health issue with chronic loneliness being found to be more harmful than smoking 15 cigarettes a day, with studies showing that it can double the risk of developing Alzheimer's and can increase the risk of premature death by up to 30 per cent. The City saw the benefits that could accrue in using the libraries to help reduce loneliness in the City. The City's Social Wellbeing Strategy has therefore been using the libraries to help break down barriers and provide safe places.

The weekly Stay and Play sessions at Shoe Lane Library have provided a meeting place for local parents, many of whom are working in the City and are far from family and friends.

When the City started working with Age Concern on a pilot project to support older women from the Bangladeshi community, the Portsoken Health and Community Centre, a satellite of Artizan Street Library, was the natural place for the new group to be based.

Creating new community spaces, much needed in the busy Square Mile, is a great way to use the libraries. In these various ways the City seeks to provide libraries, solace and resources to the residents and working day population - as well as any Liverymen who want to sign up.

First published January 2013

A major focus of all Livery Companies is to give generously to those in need. The Plaisterers have been encouraging members to consider their ability and response to the Livery's wish to increase our charitable giving. Historically the Livery Companies have been well known for their philanthropy and assistance. For some Companies money given centuries ago has increased to huge wealth and assets now - for others the sums are smaller but no less important in meeting the many needs. The latest figures show that together all the Livery Companies give away some £42 million per annum. Building on this, the Lord Mayor, Alderman Roger Gifford, has made City philanthropy an important part of his theme for the year The City in Society and said at the recent briefing to the Livery Masters, "The City has a great living legacy from our philanthropists - especially those connected to the Livery. This is a great example of City philanthropy and City stewardship; we are uniquely placed to take the long view, to benefit society now, but also to make sure those benefits are felt long into the future as well."

City Bridge Trust logo

London Bridge, a thriving hub in medieval times

A further strand in this story is the unique and interesting tale of the generosity of the City's citizens that has led to the formation of the City Bridge Trust (CBT). The City of London Corporation is the corporate trustee of this fund that gives away nearly £15 million per annum to fund charities and projects in the Greater London area (ie the City and the 32 Boroughs). I have the privilege to sit on the Trust and see so many innovative ways that people are working across London to address disadvantage.

The particular areas that the CBT fund are Accessible London (eg, £50,000 given to the Charles Dickens Museum to improve access); Bridging Communities (eg, £45,000 to Disability Rights UK to fund a leadership development programme for young disabled people); London's Environment (eg, Thames 21 received £150,000 over three years for a project officer to develop a scheme of local volunteering to improve London's waterways and the Thames); Older Londoners (eg, £20,000 paid to Haringey Carers' Centre to support older carers in

The Bridge House Estates Bridge Mark denoting ownership

Haringey); Positive Transitions to Independent Living (eg, £90,000 to SignHealth for outreach workers helping deaf women and their children affected by domestic violence); Strengthening the Third Sector (eg, the Volunteer Centre Southwark received £85,000 over two years for a volunteer development officer); Improving London's Mental Health (eg, Beat received £111,700 for Londoners who have eating disorders). In addition the Trust has occasional special projects. This year it launched Growing Localities. A fund of £2million has been set aside to celebrate the Diamond Jubilee that aims to make better use of London's green spaces, encourage community engagement, help reduce social isolation through working with others, teach people the value of biodiversity and growing food, engage people of all ages in the management of their community green space and encourage young unemployed people and other special needs groups into horticultural/market garden accredited work training or apprenticeships. For example it has awarded to Green Corridor £89,900 over two years towards the salary and project costs required to provide a horticultural training and education project for 105 young people.

The origins of the funds make an equally interesting story. Just as the Trust now serves London the fact is that for centuries London's citizens had made gifts of land and money to God and the Bridge - that is London Bridge. The Church encouraged the building of bridges and this activity was so important it was perceived to be an act of piety - a commitment to God that should be supported by the giving of alms. In 1097 William Rufus, second son of William the Conqueror, raised a special tax to help repair the wooden London Bridge. Then in 1176, during the reign of Henry II , Peter de Colechurch, a priest and head of the Fraternity of the Brethren of London Bridge, began building the first stone bridge across the River Thames. That bridge, with its 19 arches, was completed 33 years later in 1209. By the end of the 13th century the shops and houses adorning the new stone London Bridge were beginning to generate not only increased cross-river trade, but also increased taxes, rents and bequests. A significant fund began to accumulate.

Over the centuries the fund prospered mightily through strong and thrifty administration of the ever-increasing property assets both in the City and the surrounding countryside. The Bridgemasters administered the fund from the Bridge House and maximised income from a great variety of sources including, for example: "receiving tolls on carts passing over the Bridge, tolls from ships passing under the Bridge and fines for unlawful fishing from the Bridge".

In relatively recent years the charity built Blackfriars Bridge, purchased Southwark Bridge and, just over a century ago, constructed Tower Bridge. In February 2002, the Trust took over the ownership and maintenance of the new pedestrian-only Millennium Bridge.

The Trust was only used to fund expenditure on its bridges. No financial support comes from the Government or any other source, so if one of the bridges happened to collapse the charity would have to rebuild it out of its own resources. However, in the later years of the 20th Century a cy-près scheme evolved which allowed the objects of the fund to be widened, enabling any surplus monies to

The Chairman, Dhruv Patel and Deputy, Alison Gowman, meeting and working with the Mayor of London

be applied to other charitable purposes benefiting Greater London. This applies only after setting aside adequate provision for the Trust's primary purpose, which remains the provision and maintenance of the five bridges.

The Trust first began awarding grants on this wider basis in September 1995. To date nearly £200 million has been given away to good and deserving causes.

Please visit the City Bridge Trust website (www.citybridgetrust.org.uk) for more details. If you are involved in a charity that operates in Greater London in these areas then do make an application to the Trust as they are keen to hear of new organisations.

The author served as Chair of the City Bridge Trust from 2016-19 and then took up the role as Deputy Chair. The annual sums given away by the Livery Companies to charitable causes is estimated to be £67 million per annum in 2018. The City Bridge Trust have a new funding strategy that commenced in April 2018 and makes grants of approximately £20 million per annum.

41. THE CITY'S NOT SO SECRET CASH

First published July 2013

In a previous article I wrote about the City Bridge Trust, which provides a huge sum annually for charitable works in Greater London with the core monies being spent on repair of the City's bridges. In addition to that sum, the City has another large fund of assets that has grown over the centuries including endowments and donations given for example by such famous City personages as Dick Whittington. This sum, called City's Cash, is not a public fund, and is therefore not subject to public scrutiny and is not used for matters that relate to the City's role as a local authority. However, the income

Guildhall School of Music and Drama

and interest generated allows the City to provide services of importance to Greater London and the UK as well as the City.

The size of this fund has been kept confidential over the centuries. This has been a source of much criticism about the City of London and its alleged lack of transparency. During the Occupy London protest outside St Paul's, one of the elements of reform that Occupy called for was the publishing of these accounts so as to give a clear indication from the Corporation of London as to where their money is spent. However, at the end of 2012, the City published an outline of the funds and their use. The press have suggested that this publication has only been made as a result of Occupy and other critics but the City Corporation had been discussing this for some time and has now produced the summary of its position.

The bottom line is that the City's investments in this fund as at March 31st 2012 totalled £1.319 billion. This is made up of investments in freehold and leasehold properties, stocks, equities and bonds. The details are online at the City's website at www.cityoflondon.gov.uk. The annual expenditure is used as to 44% on education (the City schools and the Guildhall School of Music and Drama); 14% on open spaces, which includes the upkeep of Hampstead Heath, Epping Forest and the other 11,000 acres owned or managed by the Corporation; 11% on markets - being Billingsgate, Smithfield and the New Spitalfields market; 14% on investment and property management costs; 2% of the budget (some £3.7 million) goes towards economic development; 6% of the funds are spent towards grants and 9% of the total that is spent on City representation. Some of these categories need a bit more explanation.

The sum used for economic development entails expenditure on work that supports and promotes the City's competitiveness. One of the main aims is to increase the capacity of the wider London community and especially the neighbouring boroughs to the City of London. Thus the Economic Development Department carries out work in encouraging corporate responsibility in City firms, assisting in regeneration work as well as promoting education, training, skills development and entrepreneurship. Looking at it from a wider point of view this work also involves helping to shape legislation that affects UK businesses both in Westminster and Whitehall and also through the City's office in Brussels in the European context. The Economic Development Department works with the Lord Mayor and the Chairman of Policy and Resources in planning visits overseas and welcoming high-level inward visits from senior business and political representatives. For example, in the past year London became the centre for the Renminbi business. The City Corporation worked with HM Treasury and various leading global banks to ensure that this initiative was taken up and has been consolidated since the initial launch. There is also a large ongoing research programme that includes research into the City's competitiveness, issues such as utilities regulation and investment in new businesses. The City has launched a major project on social investment that followed on from a highly acclaimed piece of

City of London School For Girls

research. Small and medium-sized enterprises are a major part of the occupiers of the City and in the fringe boroughs and the City works hard with them in order to ensure that they have facilities, funding and support to grow.

The £8.5 million spent on grants and other activities is over and above the funds paid out through the City Bridge Trust referred to previously. With this money, for example, the City can respond to major international emergencies and has often donated funds through the Red Cross and Red Crescent to various disasters.

The last element is a sum of £12.8 million per annum towards City representation. This amount has been misconstrued as a sum that the City used to 'pay' for influence in government and elsewhere. That cannot be said to be the purpose or the aim of this funding. It is out of this sum that the Lord Mayor's programme is funded and, in particular, the 100 days abroad that the Lord Mayor spends with a series of high-profile meetings. At the same time the Chairman of Policy and Resources has a major programme of visits both inward and external and these are also funded from this sum. The City hosts many events from major national occasions such as State or guest of Government visits to other lower

City of London School

profile visits from Ministers as well as the international or national celebrations that often feature in the news. From this source the Lord Mayor's expenditure at the Mansion House is funded as well as other costs of the Sheriffs and the ceremonial events within the City. In 2012 the City played a large part in the hosting of Olympic and Paralympic countries and unusually the Lord Mayor worked throughout the summer period on this element. The City also celebrated Charles Dickens' 200th birthday, the Guild of St Bartholomew's Hospital and the City of London Special Constabulary.

The summary of information given is just that. The newspapers who commented on the publication of these details were generally approving of the bold step that the City took to publish but some still carped at the lack of full detail. The City Reform Group (a recently formed coalition of think tanks, faith groups and City businesses) said "the release of some details of the City Cash is a welcome step in the direction of the transparency and accountability (we have) been calling for".

Following your reading of this article and the associated booklet on the Corporation's website you are now equally well informed.

First published July 2013

At the start of the year the City of London gave notice to the Plaisterers that there would be a road closure of London Wall westbound between Moorgate and the Aldersgate Street rotunda for a period of eight weeks from January 7th. They informed the Hall that this would interfere with vehicular access to Plaisterers' Hall and cause some traffic delays and inconvenience. A decision had been made to close the road entirely in order to repair some damage which included damage caused to the roof of the London Wall car park which passes underneath London Wall just by the Hall. Arrangements were made for supplies to be brought into the Hall by lorry from Noble Street, which was opened up especially in order to allow the Hall and One London Wall to continue to operate. Although this was a

Road closure at King William Street

one-off incident, City users will be concerned about the numerous times that they see the roads and pavements dug up, often at short notice.

Unless there is an emergency (for example, a gas leak) any utility company who wishes to carry out works has to discuss this first with the City's Highways team. The whole process is monitored and authorised by the City of London Corporation through the City's Highways Team based in the Department of the Built Environment. Indeed with bigger schemes the discussions need to incorporate a wide range of professionals in order to ensure that any works comply with noise issues, traffic flow and other environmental matters. Traffic flow and other planned events (for

@Squarehighways Twitter feed

example, The Lord Mayor's Show), are all considered so as to ensure that the works are carried out with the least inconvenience to everyone. Since January 2010 the City have operated a permit scheme that means all contractors have to apply for a permit to dig up the highway. A fee is charged and conditions can be attached so that a failure to comply will result in a fine and enforcement steps being taken. However, all statutory utility companies have a legal right to dig up roads and footways in order to maintain their equipment and to provide new supplies. This is part and parcel of being a vibrant and

Road works in Cannon Street

growing City. When the Corporation becomes aware of some intended works they invite any other utility companies to take advantage of the road closure and works so as to share the disruption time and share the work that has been done to open up the relevant pipe or trench. When the City was forced to close the whole of the Bank junction over a weekend period last year for urgent works they alerted all the other utilities who came in and carried out similar works, which saved approximately 100 working days when all or part of that junction might have been closed. This is the ideal because it saves road closure time and disruption and ensures collaborative working. However, there is no ability for the City or any other local authority to force these utility companies to work together and there can be health and safety complications resulting from too many contractors working in one area at the same time!

Any permit granted by the Corporation has a time limit that should be displayed on the notice pinned to the fencing. If the contractor overruns then a criminal offence is committed and a fixed penalty notice can be issued. However, the contractor can ask for permit extensions. The fine is up to £500 per occasion and additionally there can be daily charges of between £250 and £5,000 per day. Believe you me, the City do issue these notices. But the City can exercise judgment in the time that the road is closed since any planned closures do require formal traffic management (regulation) orders. The City has to consider carefully all of the persons involved including residents, businesses and other traffic. Most of the temporary road closures need to be advertised, for example, in the local press and by way of bulletins on the City website and on street notices.

Sometimes it can seem that an area has been opened up with Heras fencing (used mostly around building sites and requiring a licence) or other barriers erected but no work has been carried out for some time. It is sometimes due to the fact that works have to be left for concrete or asphalt to harden. Sometimes, the sensitivity of the location will limit the time of day that noisy works can take place. With the new permit system it does mean that contractors will not want to overrun their time-scale and the City tries to ensure that they give a realistic time-scale in the first instance.

The City expects that anyone undertaking this work (usually utility companies) puts in place a clear and robust communication strategy before starting the works as well as considering measures to minimise the duration of the works - for example by using rapid hardening concrete where possible.

It can sometimes seem that the same street is being dug up time after time. Certainly it is one of the most frequent complaints that members of the Common Council receive. People complain because of the repeated noise and disruption as well as the apparent waste of money on re-pouring concrete or relaying flagstones seems to be disproportionate to whatever benefit is gained. However, the City as one of the World's leading business centres has a large amount of underground cabling and pipes owned by different companies and each company will have its own pressure from customers to supplement, repair or replace their network. Despite the fact that the City tries to alert other utilities to a road closure or other works being carried out, the company may not always know that works are required to the buildings next door in time to co-ordinate the collaborative working. City businesses, like other businesses, can be last minute and demanding. Each year the City issues about 6,000 permits authorising street works to take place in the square mile. About 400 are refused for a variety of reasons. About one third of the permits relate to work that the City itself wants to carry out. The City is keen to improve the road network and use the opportunity of new buildings or developments to improve areas.

Every week the City Corporation issues a traffic management bulletin. This sets out the roads that are closed or where works are going to be carried out. This includes carriageway works, building works, mobile cranes in place, street enhancement and lighting installations. This also gives ongoing and advance information about works or events that are known including particular reference to Crossrail.

As part of the wider communication strategy the Highways team publishes Streets Ahead, a quarterly newsletter with updates of works and planned activities and provides live daily broadcasts on Twitter: "@ squarehighways". You can subscribe or link in to these as part of the general public.

This explanation won't prevent the street works being carried out but will allow you some understanding of the parameters of control that the City of London Corporation have and the way in which they seek to control and minimise disruptions.

First published July 2014

The 25th July 2014 sees the Royal Marines exercise their privileged right to march through the City of London. This is a public event and so all are invited to come out onto the streets to watch and support our affiliated troops. But what does this mean? Surely all military units can (if ordered) march through any town or City in the UK? That is true … except in the City of London.

The City's unusual position in this respect goes back to 1327 when King Edward III granted a Charter to the Mayor and Commonalty of London which provided that no Citizen should be compelled to go

Plaques denoting the Privileged Regiments in Great Hall Guildhall

to War. It thus followed that recruiting or impressment could not be conducted by the Crown within the City, and this was repeated in all the Militia enactments from the time of the Restoration onwards.

In 1769, in assertion of the City's established rights to refuse to permit anything which savoured of Military intrusion, the Lord Mayor complained to the Secretary-at-War that a Detachment of Guards, returning to the Tower after suppressing a Spitalfields riot outside the City's walls, had marched through the City "with drums beating, fifes playing and generally making a warlike appearance which raised in the minds of peaceable Citizens the idea of a Town garrisoned by Regular troops". His lordship thus demanded to know by whose orders this unusual procedure took place. The Secretary-at-War, in reply, gave it as his opinion that no troops should march through the City in the manner described without previous notice to the Lord Mayor. These rights were challenged in 1842, but the Law Officers upheld the long established common law right of the Lord Mayor and Citizens to close the City's gates against entry by the Sovereign's troops.

And so to this day, whenever a party of the Armed Forces desires to enter the City, the Lord Mayor's permission is obtained. If, by chance or emergency, this is not done an apology is sent to the Lord Mayor. Such is the unique 'Privilege' of the City of London; a survival of the realities of the medieval ages.

No Regiment has the unrestricted right to march through the City and none has had the 'Freedom' conferred upon it, which is, of course, exclusive to individuals. In that respect it is interesting to note that all members of the City Imperial Volunteers were made Freemen upon their departure to the Boer War. The Court of Common Council resolved on 20th December 1899 "That the Freedom of this City be presented to every Volunteer joining The City of London Volunteer Force, for service in South Africa, as a recognition of his patriotic conduct".

Certain Regiments have acquired the 'Privilege' of marching in this special manner; subject always to their having given prior notice to the Lord Mayor of their intention to do so. How this privilege came about can be guaranteed to start an argument in any Regimental Mess!

In respect of the Royal Marines it serves to review a short bit of history. In 1664 the Privy Council met and troops were commandeered 'and prepared for sea service'. A warrant was granted to recruit in the City with the Lord Mayor's consent. The recruits were to be drawn mainly from the trained band of the City who were trained to defend the City in times of trouble. Other warrants were repeated over the next century. Indeed, despite the general rules exempting the City's citizens, it became customary to recruit the Admiral's Regiment in the City. This presumption was supported by the famous case in 1746 when a party of Marines beating along Cheapside was required to desist by a Magistrate, who was in fact an Alderman. Upon being told by the Officer Commanding the Party "Sir, we are Marines", the Alderman apologised and begged them to continue!

Pikemen and Musketeers parading in the Lord Mayor's Show

The Tercentenary of the Royal Marines was celebrated in 1964 with a reception in Guildhall and the Tercentenary Unit marched through the City and were inspected by the Lord Mayor. The strengthening of the link was made in 1974 when the association with St Lawrence Jewry was formed and the church (next to the Guildhall and with its own proximate parade ground in Guildhall Yard) was signed.

It is interesting to note that in 1924 certain Regiments not on the City's list claimed the 'Privilege'. After a great deal of correspondence in the

Royal Marines marching in the City

press, and some heated arguments in the Court of Common Council an inquiry was set up.

As a result the Privilege was confirmed in the case of the Royal Marines, the Buffs, the Grenadier Guards and the Royal Fusiliers. Surprisingly enough it would seem, from the Lord Mayor's reply of 13th October 1942, that the Honourable Artillery Company had never been considered by City authorities to be one of the Privileged Regiments for, instead of confirming the claim to the right, the Lord Mayor notified the Commanding Officer that the Privilege would in future be extended to his Regiment. And so a practice, which for many years had been based upon ancient usage only, now became officially recognised.

From papers given to the Guildhall Historical Association by Deputy John Trevor Yates MBE, 29 September 1981 and Alderman Sir Ronald Laurence Gardner-Thorpe GBE, TD, DCL, DH, 30 July 1985

44. CONGESTION IN THE CITY

First published January 2017

As the New Year begins this article is not a nod to all the possible colds and chest infections that might be going around but is rather about the clogging of the City's arteries - the road network. If you have complained recently about the time it took you to get to Plaisterers' Hall then you are just one of those many who are concerned about the creaking infrastructure.

Believe it or not the City Corporation is also very concerned as blocked and slow roads cause damage to the City's businesses and our reputation as a modern and competitive global City. This has been escalated to a main issue for discussion and action by the City Corporation and these are some of the issues being considered by the senior Committees and decision makers.

First it must be acknowledged that current major infrastructure projects such as Crossrail and the Cycle Super Highway, along with the highest level of development activity for many years, have increased the demand on the highway network's capacity. The London Assembly Transport Committee is also carrying out an investigation into congestion as the issue is London wide. Let's hope for joined-up thinking and outcomes.

There is a range of measures that might be introduced or strengthened to improve traffic flow. The main ways to improve traffic movement can be summarised as managing the streets more effectively, spreading the length of time over which vehicles use the City and, most importantly, reducing the amount of traffic in the City to a level that the City community finds acceptable.

A recent City report has proposed the following three-pronged approach to congestion. First, to

Busy overcrowded Bank Junction

make representations for a London-wide policy change, for example, changes to the congestion charge. Second, to develop a range of strategic and proactive measures to improve traffic flow in the short to medium term, for example, reducing the number and changing the time of goods vehicle arrivals, tackling perceived congestion hot spots such as Bank Junction. Thirdly, the use of reactive mitigation - ie the close monitoring of our network and speedy response to issues with robust enforcement.

This may sound like a lot of political hot air - but if the issue were easy to solve then it would have happened by now. Consideration has to be given to the need for sufficient space for the residents, visitors and workers in the City to move around safely and efficiently. But as the likely future demand is to build another 1.15 million square meters of office floorspace; planned to accommodate a further 58,000 workers, then there is clearly a growing need for circulation of ever larger numbers. Other competing interests are the growing number of cyclists and pedestrians who are involved in 83% of all road accidents. A City that looks jumbled and overcrowded is not pleasant and the aim is to create 'places' within the City that add to its character and wellbeing which along with improving the air quality, is critical for all. London is failing its international commitments and bad air quality is a significant cause of deaths and shortened lives across the capital.

What is the makeup of the current traffic on our roads? Cars and taxis make up almost 50% of traffic movements. Goods vehicles of various sizes make up some 22% of all traffic movements and their associated loading and unloading can also add to congestion. Buses and coaches are 5% and

Quiet car free Bank Junction

the rest is 8% motorcycles and 16% pedal cycles. What would you do to limit or control all of these modes of transport?

The ideas being considered are:

- Increasing the congestion charge - when it was first introduced in 2003 it had an impact that has now lessened and so an increase or extension of the zone might assist in boosting a further fall in traffic numbers.
- Limiting the traffic into the City by way of the traffic lights that are controlled across London by Transport for London.
- Reducing bus numbers - many of the bus routes are determined historically by reference to the need for horses to stop at watering troughs. This is no longer relevant!
- Bridge tolls across the London bridges. Rest assured this was rejected by the committees to date!
- Implementing 'Smart City' ideas to use technology to solve the issues by warning of congestion ahead in real time and at the same time operating the traffic lights to allow greater and lesser flows depending on surrounding traffic and blockages. Technology can also lead to identifying parking spaces and preventing crawling around the streets to find a space with the ultimate in electric cars being clean and smart to use.
- Managing freight deliveries around the clock (subject to residential impact of noise and disturbance) and consolidating deliveries to offices that have proliferated with online purchasing and repeated drop offs at offices to the many staff inside.
- Better management of road works and utilities and combining road disruption with several operators all working at the same time and saving further digging up of the roads.

Detailed plans for a calmer slower London Wall

One significant project that is still in the committee decision phase is to re-plan the Bank Junction, making it less frenetic and reducing the number of road accidents at the junction. A long-term solution might take several years to arrange and implement but the interim plan is to limit access to Bank Junction between 7am and 7pm to pedestrians, pedal cycles and buses only. This will be a temporary plan for 18 months in order to assess the impact. All the modelling that has been carried out shows that it will ensure a significant reduction in road casualties; will be neutral or slightly positive to traffic journey times and will benefit the bus services in the area. The most vocal opposition comes from the taxi trade who fear the worst. However, the model shows that if taxis are included there will be none of the benefits suggested. The battle is still playing out across the City's committees - but everyone agrees that something needs to be done.

The pilot scheme to reduce vehicular traffic at Bank Junction was successful and was made permanent by Order of the Court of Common Council on September 13th 2018. Further changes at Bank Junction and elsewhere are under consideration and The City of London has been consulting on a new Transport Strategy and a new Local Plan.
The Transport Strategy was approved by the Court of Common Council on May 23rd 2019. This includes proposals to prioritise the needs of people walking, make streets more accessible and deliver world-class public realm; eliminating death and serious injuries through the promotion of safer streets and reducing traffic speeds; enabling more people to cycle with confidence and improving air quality and enabling the switch to zero emission capable vehicles.
The City Corporation set up a network of businesses that are interested in issues around active travel and to promote walking and cycling in the City. This is called the Active City Network and is chaired by the author. The network produces a best practice guide each year to share ideas of helping staff and businesses to use active travel to be healthier and to travel safely in the City.

Active City Network

First published May 2016

Logo of the City of London Office in Brussels

It is important that this article steers a neutral course with regard to the up and coming EU referendum. However, it is an opportunity to explain the current links that the City of London Corporation has set up with the EU states and Brussels. It may not be known widely that the City has had an office in Brussels since 2004 and, at the end of 2015, appointed a new senior representative for the City in Europe.

The purpose of the City office in Brussels was to strengthen relations between the City of London and EU institutions. The office in Brussels represents the needs of an international financial marketplace. It liaises between the City and both the EU institutions and Member States - strengthening dialogue between them.

The City office focuses on cross-sectoral issues in which pan-EU policy making could affect the competitiveness of international financial services and therefore the EU's economic growth. It facilitates wider City contacts by staging networking events and briefing meetings with MEPs, European Commission officials and Member States' representatives.

The strategic aims of the office are:

- To help shape the evolution of more effective financial services within the EU - assisting in the creation of a coherent strategy for future growth and development of the single market for financial services.
- To promote the interests of the wider City as a key international marketplace - acting as a focal point in Brussels for UK-based international financial services through informal contacts with decision makers.
- To act as a channel for regular communication between EU officials and MEPs and the international financial services community on matters of collective interest.

In September 2015 the City of London Corporation appointed the former Minister of State for Foreign Affairs, Jeremy Browne, as Special Representative for the City. He will look to enhance the UK's financial and professional services industry's engagement with EU institutions and across Member States. Jeremy's remit will include:

- Engaging with the most senior EU policy makers and officials ensuring that the City Corporation remains fully engaged in EU policy making. This will include the European Commission's Investment Plan and the development of an EU Capital Markets Union.
- Providing insight to senior leaders of financial and professional services firms on EU policy development.
- Explaining the value to senior EU opinion formers of London's role as Europe's international financial centre and how this supports EU-wide economic growth and job creation.
- Influencing the development of relevant EU financial services and related policy dossiers.
- Ensuring that the City's voice is heard in Brussels ahead of the UK referendum on EU membership.

Jeremy Browne said on his appointment that "The financial and professional services sector is one of the real strengths of the UK's economy, supporting jobs and growth across the country. I look forward to representing the City in Brussels, ensuring it is more engaged there and in Member States, and am delighted to be taking on this new role."

At his first official function he spoke about the issues at stake. He said that "Europe cannot afford to be complacent in the quest for economic growth and stability," and went on to praise the City of London as the "embodiment" of the European ideal and as a real "European asset."

He said: "Europe is a relatively prosperous continent but our share of the overall global economy will shrink significantly in the coming decades. We face much more intense competition. Economic power is no longer concentrated in a small number of industrialised nations. We cannot afford to be complacent, assuming that our success in the past gives us a right to be successful in the future.

"There is no divine decree that determines that the premier international financial centre must be located in Europe. The remarkable status of the City of London is built on solid historical foundations: the rule of law; a welcoming business environment; political stability and moderation; a free and inquisitive civic culture; and the English language.

City envoy Jeremy Browne

"But it is also the product of the mindset that Britain - and Europe as a whole - will require in order to be prosperous and globally relevant. These features exist in abundance in the City of London: innovation and creativity; embracing change; industrious; internationalist.

"It is easy to talk about the European ideal; the City of London is the actual embodiment of it. Financial institutions from across our continent and the wider world; employees selected on the basis of talent rather than nationality; customers from every corner of the planet. This amazing creation is a model of organic growth, not central planning, fostered in the unique environment of London: a great European city. It is living proof that the people of Europe can come together to be more than the sum of their parts."

Over the last six months or so Jeremy has visited all the member states ensuring that they know about the City and its work and to gauge their issues with the City and UK. These visitations enhance those of the Lord Mayor who will visit those countries as they take up the EU Presidency (presently the Netherlands but changing to Slovakia on July 1st). Additionally the Chairman of Policy and Resources makes frequent visits to Brussels and other EU countries.

Like it or not the EU are our nearest neighbours and the City's financial and global outlook is enhanced by our proximity and ease of business and travel. But it all may change on 23 June!

The EU referendum outcome was that by a vote of 52% to 48%, Britain should leave the EU. After a change of Prime Minister and snap General Election, the new Prime Minister, Mrs Theresa May, triggered Article 50 in March 2017 with a view to the UK leaving the EU on 29th March 2019. At that time no agreement had been reached in Parliament as to the terms of the exit and an extension was agreed. Mrs May resigned as Prime Minister in June 2019, triggering an election for a new leader of the Conservative Party. At the time of going to press, this is not resolved. The City of London Corporation has been liaising with businesses and Government in order to support the best outcome for financial services and, in particular, argued for a clear transition to ensure that business could have time adapt to the change; agree the best deal on free trade for Britain and the EU27 and support for the best talent to be allowed to live and work in the UK in order to allow the UK's business and financial services to thrive.

Nick Collier was appointed as the City's new representative in Brussels in early 2019.

First published July 2016

Just across the road from Plaisterers' Hall is the Museum of London. So near and yet so far - when did you last visit this treasure trove and paean of praise to our capital City? Let's hope that this article will revive your interest in things historical and help you to understand the dynamic City that we love and support.

Aerial shot of the current Museum site near to Plaisterers' Hall

Even a Museum has its own history and the Museum of London was formed with that new name in 1963-4 when the City Corporation agreed to merge its own Guildhall Museum (housed in the Guildhall and Royal Exchange and founded in 1826) with the London Museum (owned by the then London County Council). The merged museum became the Museum of London. That historic link is important because the main sponsors of the Museum are the City of London Corporation and the Greater London Authority. Governors are appointed from each of the sponsoring bodies and liaison over strategic matters takes place at the highest level between these two important London Governing bodies.

The enhanced Museum was opened in December 1976 as part of the Barbican Estate. The architects were Philip Powell and Hidalgo Moya who adopted an innovative approach to museum design, whereby the galleries were laid out so that there was only one route through the museum - from the prehistoric period to the modern galleries. You can't get lost. Despite several expert and award-winning changes over the years its current site clearly has limitations and plans to refurbish or rebuild concluded with the idea to move entirely to a site at West Smithfield, being the unused part of the Smithfield meat market. The site is owned the City Corporation and is in a conservation area. An architectural competition has been undertaken and the jury of Governors and external advisers are seeking to decide the architect to choose for this momentous role. The competition plans are on display in the Museum but the result of

the jury will be announced during July and so you are likely to be hearing a lot more about the museum during this month.

What can you see? It is certainly worth visiting in its present location. The Museum of London tells the story of the capital from its first settlers to modern times. The unfolding galleries vividly tell the story of the city and its people. Starting in 450,000BC right up to modern displays about Punk and the Cauldron from the opening ceremony of the Olympics in 2012. From Roman settlement to the development of Canary Wharf, the long history of the capital as a port is revealed through stories of trade, migration and commerce.

The new galleries place a renewed emphasis on contemporary London and contemporary collecting. "World City" is the gallery that tells London's story from 1950 to the present day. Fashion looms large here - from formal suits of the 1950s, through to the Mary Quant dresses of the swinging 1960s, hippy chic in the 1970s and the bondage trousers and ripped T-shirts of the punk era. Fashion comes right up to date with a pashmina from Alexander McQueen's 2008 collection. The main hall contains an elliptical LED curtain where the work of up-and-coming young

Museum Director Sharon Ament at the site of the new Museum in Smithfield

The cauldron of petals created for the London Olympics 2012

filmmakers is screened in a bi-annual Museum of London Film Commission, in association with Film London. Here, of course, you can see the Lord Mayor's Coach up close and the surrounding gallery tells a more Livery and Civic-focused story that will appeal to Plaisterers.

The London Wall site receives over a million visitors each year and holds the largest archaeological archive in Europe, caring for more than two million objects in the collections. Inevitably there is a café and restaurant immediately adjacent and a very well-stocked shop for London objects, books and unique limited edition artefacts that are great gifts and presents.

There is a lot of storage needed. In the Museum of London Archaeological Archive there is information from excavations in London over the past 100 years. You can imagine how much was added after the Second World War as bombsites revealed many ancient finds and now many new developments involve further digging and research and added objects to the list. The Archive is held at Mortimer Wheeler House in Hackney.

Part of the Archaeological Archive is the Centre for Human Bioarchaeology which curates and researches skeletal remains. This may seem slightly ghoulish but the information and knowledge gained from this research has proved invaluable.

The last piece of the jigsaw is the Museum of London Docklands. The port and river collection is displayed at the Museum of London Docklands in a 200-year-old warehouse located close to the River Thames. Rather dwarfed by the tall office buildings, it is an oasis of culture, history and families.

The Museum has a fabulous and informative website (www.museumoflondon.org.uk) that gives full details of the many events that take place over and above the general collection and special exhibitions. There are workshops for people of all ages, sleepovers, walks and talks.

A replica 17th century fire engine made for the Fire Fire exhibition

© Museum of London

At the end of July a major exhibition called Fire! Fire! opens (23 July to 17 April). This will tell the story of the Great Fire in 1666 - a symbolic turning point in the history of the capital and pivotal in the way that London recreated itself out of both the destruction of the buildings but also the deaths from the Great Plague beforehand. The Museum is free to enter but the exhibition has a small charge. It is well worth the visit - especially with children.

The support and financial contribution that the City of London Corporation makes to the Museum is just one part of the City's support to the Cultural Hub, the brand name that the City has given to the cultural and educational institutions based around the Barbican area. The Museum plays an important role and even when it moves to Smithfield this is just a natural extension of the physical area and a relocation to an area so redolent of and steeped in the history of this City.

The architects chosen to design the new Museum are Stanton Williams with Asif Khan and Julian Harrap. The Museum of London is the chosen charity of the year for the Plaisterers' Livery 2019-20.

47. THE CITY'S WHOLESALE MARKETS

First published March 2019

I t may surprise some that the City of London Corporation is the market authority for three major wholesale food markets. Indeed, the City was given this right by charter in 1327. Until 30 years ago all were located in the Square Mile: Billingsgate, Spitalfields and Smithfield markets. Each are still extant and trading but have now changed either location or clientele. However, all are thriving and part of the rich pattern of the City's life.

Billingsgate Market

As even the busiest of City or Canary Wharf workers are waking and entering their business zones; inside these markets many traders in white or brown coats are already busy and in most cases ready to close up shop for the day.

These markets have existed variously since the 14th century and still thrive today. Although now only Smithfield is actually in the square mile, the old buildings of Billingsgate and Spitalfields still have historic resonance and new uses to make them live again in a new age.

Billingsgate is the UK's largest inland fish market, located in the shadow of Canary Wharf.

Fish comes here from all round the UK: from Aberdeen and Grimsby, Brixham and the Shetland Isles, Whitstable and Lowestoft: coley and cod, sea bream and salmon, tiger-striped mackerel and scallops in the shell. Some stalls specialise in 'exotics' - species of fish from faraway: redfish, milkfish, catfish, kingfish, needle fish, barracuda, croaker, tilapia, and frozen breeze-blocks of squid. The clientele is as diverse as the products with many seeking specific food types to serve in venues from restaurants and cafes to catering businesses and hotels - many hail from diverse ethnic communities who are seeking special food or a taste of their home produce.

Billingsgate moved from its Thameside home on Lower Thames Street to the Docklands in 1982. Some 25,000 tonnes of fish a year (almost 100 tonnes a day), pass through on the way from the sea to the plate. Trading starts on the ringing of a bell at 4am. There are over 100 stalls and shops that sell their wares and a freezer store the size of a football pitch holds the stock in between sales.

Billingsgate was known as Blynesgate and Byllynsgate before the name settled into its present form. The origin of the name is unclear and could refer to a watergate at the south side of the City where goods were landed - perhaps owned by a man named Biling - or it may have originated with Belin (400BC) an ancient King of the period.

Billingsgate was originally a general market for corn, coal, iron, wine, salt, pottery, fish and miscellaneous goods and does not seem to have become associated exclusively with the fish trade until the sixteenth century.

In 1699 an Act of Parliament was passed making it "a free and open market for all sorts of fish whatsoever". The only exception to this was the sale of eels, which was restricted to Dutch fishermen whose boats were moored in the Thames. This was because they had helped feed the people of London during the Great Fire.

The Billingsgate Seafood Training School is located at the Market and can provide tailor-made classroom-based courses and demonstrations in fish recognition, knife skills, presentation, cooking and nutrition.

The Fishmongers' Livery has a continuing historic link with the Market and undertakes the role of inspectors at the market. A section in the Act of Parliament that moved the market transferred the Livery Company's powers to the new site, and the Company has continued to maintain at its own expense, a small team of inspectors whose daily work ensures the high quality of seafood sold at Billingsgate. The inspectors are also charged with responsibilities under the Salmon and Freshwater Fisheries Act and the Shellfish Act and they are appointed by Defra as Sea Fisheries Officers. These other duties help to ensure that only seafood that is caught legally is allowed to be sold on the market.

Fruit at Spitalfields Market

New Spitalfields is the UK's largest wholesale fruit and vegetable market, located in Leyton, close to the Olympic site. As London's premier horticultural market, Spitalfields Market offers the widest range of fruit, vegetables and flowers and there are many specialist traders in exotic fruit and vegetables. This gives the greatest choice of these products of any market in Europe. New Spitalfields occupies an area of over 31 acres and has great access to transport systems across London and the UK as well as extensive parking for the many lorries and vehicles visiting daily. Over 100 traders work in the new market and needless to say that they have attracted some related businesses with catering supply companies and fruit importers vying for space in the vicinity.

The old site on the north east of the City has itself been repurposed as a craft market with a buzzing and vibrant 'cool' community feel. There had been a market on this site for over 350 years since King Charles I gave a licence for flesh, fowl and roots to be sold on Spittle Fields in 1638. At the time, this was a rural area on the eastern outskirts of London. The rights to a market seems to have lapsed during the Cromwellian era, but the market was re-founded in 1682 by King Charles II in order to feed the burgeoning population of a new suburb. The existing buildings were built by the City Corporation in the 1880s to service the wholesale market.

At the end of the 20th century, there was a dispute between the owners, the City of London Corporation and local residents about local redevelopment. The Corporation won, and now a Norman Foster-designed office block surrounds the western side of the site, after two-thirds of the historic market were rebuilt. The original Victorian buildings and the market hall and roof have been restored and Spitalfields is now one of the major markets in London. The market square is a popular fashion, arts and crafts, food and general market, open seven days a week, and it is particularly busy at weekends.

Smithfield, or London Central Markets as it is officially known, is the only wholesale Market that remains located on its original site within the Square Mile. The site is the location of the market for over 1,000 years. As London grew around the livestock market, Smithfield became increasingly controversial, not just for what one Victorian campaigner described as the "cruelty, filth, effluvia, pestilence, impiety, horrid language, danger, disgusting and shuddering sights" of the market itself, but also thanks to the chaos caused by driving animals through the narrow streets. A new cattle market was opened in 1855 in Islington, and Smithfield was re-established as a meat market, with carcasses delivered by underground railway. The iconic East and West Market Buildings were completed in 1868 and the trade in livestock and meat continued. These buildings were renovated in the 1990s to meet current hygiene standards, costing more than £70 million.

The current traders at Smithfield today have successfully battled against redevelopment of one kind or another. The now-disused General Market, alongside Farringdon Road, is earmarked for the relocation of the Museum of London, but the Victorian East and West Markets and the 20th-century Poultry Market are all listed, severely limiting the scope for profitable redevelopment.

Twenty years ago, says David Smith, Director of Markets and Consumer Protection at City of London

Smithfield Market

Corporation, wholesale markets looked like a spent force, a relic from a pre-modern era. Supermarkets were establishing their own supply chains and their own warehouses on the edge of London; the wholesale markets' niche would only become narrower. Three factors threw the markets a lifeline: one was London's phenomenal boom in dining out, encompassing everything from opulent Michelin aspirants to inventive street food pop-ups. A city whose food had traditionally served as the butt of other people's jokes became one of the world's great dining destinations.

Another factor was immigration: supermarkets work at scale but the choice they offer is heavily circumscribed. International food aisles have been outpaced by the growth in specialist suppliers of everything from Chinese greens to curry leaves; Polish sausage to pomfret. At Billingsgate alone, 'exotics' are now reckoned to make up 40 per cent of turnover. New Londoners have revitalised the city's markets as well as its cuisine.

The third factor was a change in food-buying culture and a resurgence of middle-class interest in authenticity and provenance. The markets increasingly operate at the edge of

The City of London Griffin over the entrance to Smithfield Market

mainstream consumption, providing specialities for minority cuisines and exquisite ingredients for epicureans, as well as acting as a secondary market for produce that is just a little too gnarly and imperfect for the supermarkets' exacting aesthetic standards.

The latest twist in the story of these markets is that the City Corporation is now seeking to move all three markets to a new purpose-built site - meaning that Smithfield would leave the City as well. Finding a site to house all three markets with good transport access is not easy but plans are afoot and press reports keep us up to date.

Meanwhile, all three markets are open to the public to visit and all are worth the very early morning start to enjoy traditional City trading and grab a bargain.

48. WHY ALL THE FUSS NOW ABOUT THE GREAT FIRE?

First published September 2016

The year 1666 is one that all school children recall - now enshrined in the national curriculum Key Stage 1. Indeed as you are reading this article in early September 2016 you will be surrounded by myriad commemorations concentrated on the weekend of September 2-4 (the actual days of the fire) but with other events lasting over the whole of 2016.

Drawing of the Great Fire of London 1666

It is not surprising that for the City of London this is a seminal point in its history and recreation. Dr Simon Thurley calls it one of the Five Catastrophes that made London. So many organisations refer to it - our own Plaisterers included - as the time that our Hall was destroyed (and not the only time by fire). Blue plaques abound recalling the site of … 'destroyed by the Great Fire'. Some 83% of the physical City was destroyed but fewer than 10 people actually died at the time. Thurley states: "In 1550, most Londoners lived in the Square Mile; by 1700, most Londoners lived outside it. Of the 13,500 houses burnt in the Great Fire, only around 4,000 were rebuilt. And many of the ones that were rebuilt, the speculative developers found very hard to let because, even after the Fire, the city was crowded and polluted. Living there was expensive and vexatious and downright hard work, as a disproportionate number of people had to serve on the top-heavy governance of 26 wards, 242 precincts, and over 100 parishes - an incredibly cumbersome, top-heavy governance."

So let's see what the City is doing to remember the Great Fire. The Museum of London is curating the Fire! Fire! Exhibition until April 17th 2017. The Museum has been the repository of the story and has created an interactive exhibition especially aimed at families but also telling personal stories of the people involved. A highlight of the display is a replica 17th-century fire engine that has been rebuilt with traditional stills by Croford's, a historic coachmaker, supported by three Livery Companies - the Coopers, Grocers and Joiners and Ceilers.

St Paul's - Christopher Wren's triumph - is hosting a series of events and services. Still to come here is a debate on September 13th addressing questions such as what makes London a resilient city that can

A line of dominos marked the route of the Great Fire in commemorations 2016 (running through Dowgate Ward)

so successfully stand the test of time? The sermons on the four Sundays in September at 11am follow a theme of resurgence under the title Out of the Ashes.

The City's own institutions are presenting exhibitions at the Guildhall Library, London Metropolitan Archives and City Heritage Gallery for most of 2016. October and November see productions of the Great Fire Opera at The Temple Church and a play, Fire and Phoenix, at the Bridewell Theatre.

The imminent weekend of September 2-4 will unveil some exciting events that are still developing. On September 3rd a series of person-sized dominoes will mark the route of the fire and be set off across a six-kilometre run around the route of the fire in the City. Then on the evening of Sunday September 4th a wooden model of the medieval City will be floated on barges near Blackfriars Bridge and set alight to display a poignant image of our old City destroyed. Details are being released nearer the time and other events may evolve.

If you still feel you are lacking the basics and real truth of the story (and not the myths and misunderstandings or deliberate propaganda of the age) I would refer you to the recent Gresham Lecture by Dr Stephen Porter. I provide on the following pages, a précis of the start and it is available in full online at www.gresham.ac.uk.

"The Great Fire of London began innocuously enough as a fire at the premises of the baker Thomas Farriner in Pudding Lane during the early hours of Sunday 2 September 1666. Farriner was understandably reluctant to bear the responsibility for so great a disaster and insisted that it was not because of his negligence. He claimed that the fire in the oven of his bakehouse had been extinguished at about 10pm the previous evening... But it was his practice to place a stock of fuel next to the oven, so that it should be dry enough to re-light the fire in the morning, and according to one account it was actually in the oven. Farriner's fire should have been just one of those blazes which occurred from time to time in any community, where fires were lit for warmth, cooking, in furnaces, ovens and stoves, with candles for light, and fire carried from place to place to avoid the need to kindle a new one. The risk was greater in an urban environment because the density of buildings made it difficult to isolate a fire. But with a prompt and well-organised response fires were generally put out without great loss and the flames at Farriner's should have been extinguished quite quickly.

All urban communities took steps to minimize the risks of destructive blazes, through control of the building materials... At the end of the 16th century John Stow attributed the absence of large-scale fires in the City to that policy. The bulk of the houses were timber-framed, with lath-and-plaster infilling, standing several storeys high in the main streets, with the upper stories jettied forwards... Timber building was in decline as brick became the fashionable material; its use was stipulated in building regulations

The Museum of London's exhibition logo

issued by successive governments from 1580, which also imposed minimum standards of construction and prohibited the subdivision of houses. Those issued in 1620 addressed the use of timber and the congestion of buildings and specified that the upper storeys should not project outwards above the street. An Act of Parliament of 1657, that was designed to perk up the policy, required that new buildings should be 'built with Brick or Stone, or both, and straight up, without butting or jetting out into the Street, Lane or place'...

Despite all of that, the blaze in Farriner's bakehouse was not quenched... Effective fire-fighting depends on the speed and decisiveness of the response as soon as the alarm is raised, before the fire can develop. In that respect, the conditions in early September 1666 were against the fire-fighters. It had been a hot, dry summer across much of Europe and in England both July and August were warmer than any of the corresponding months during the previous seven years, literally since records began... and over the days when the fire blazed there was a strong gale blowing from the east, whipping in across the estuary, which fanned the flames.

Added to the problems caused by the high wind was the fact that this part of the City was a difficult one in which to deal with a major fire. Pudding Lane ran northwards from Thames Street to East Cheap in an area of narrow streets and alleys 'close built with wooden pitched houses'. Many of the occupiers were tradesmen dealing in flammable goods relating to shipping and sea-borne commerce. The excavation of a cellar in Pudding Lane has shown that barrels of pitch, a caulking agent, were stored there and that the building above was timber-framed with a tiled roof. Those premises were typical of the Thames Street area, which contained 'old paper buildings and the most combustible matter of Tarr, Pitch, Hemp, Rosen, and Flax', while the nearby wharves were stacked with timber and coal.

... the flames gradually took hold of the nearby premises After the alarm had been raised - apparently with 'a great noise of drums' - the Lord Mayor, Sir Thomas Bludworth, was called to the scene from his house in Aldersgate, and, having assessed the situation, was said to have remarked that 'a woman might

A model of London constructed from timber, with the old St Paul's, was burned on the Thames as part of the Great Fire commemorations

piss it out'. Whether he did say that or not, it was held against him thereafter, as was the allegation that he refused to order the demolition of nearby properties to create a fire-break - the common practice in such an emergency - reportedly asking "when the houses have been brought down, who shall pay the charge of rebuilding them?"… a later judgement was that by the time that fifteen or sixteen houses had caught fire, the chance of containing the blaze in the strong wind had already passed.

That wind drove the flames through the buildings, creating heat, smoke, ash and flying debris which made fire-fighting almost impossibly difficult. The fire-fighters' problems were exacerbated by the crowded streets as the citizens moved their possessions to safety, on foot, by cart, by whatever means they could find. Initially, those whose houses were threatened moved their goods relatively short distances, only to realise fairly quickly that they had to take them further away. As the area threatened with destruction grew, so did the number of people whose premises were endangered. The Thames was a possible escape route for those living close to the waterfront and Pepys described it as full of lighters and boats loaded with their belongings, while other goods were floating in the water. John Evelyn saw the river 'coverd with goods floating, all the barges & boates laden with what some had time & courage to save'. The flames mostly drove westwards, but also made progress northwards and, more slowly because against the wind, eastwards, towards the Tower, so that houses on Tower Hill were demolished as a precaution. The king ordered the establishment of eight fire-posts around the conflagration from which the fire-fighting would be co-ordinated, and he put the Duke of York in overall control. But the fire-post in Coleman Street had to be abandoned as the flames threatened. There was no stopping the fires with the means and manpower available, and those who lived within the threatened area would surely have been more concerned about their house and possessions than with fire-fighting. Only when the wind dropped, on the Wednesday, could the fires be brought under control and then quenched."

First published January 2019

I t is an excellent urban myth that a freeman of the City of London can take their sheep across London Bridge. You may be thinking that you should do this at some stage. Well, since 2013 you have been able to do so courtesy of the Worshipful Company of Woolmen. But where does this idea stem from? The origin is that freemen of the City in the middle ages did not need to pay a toll to bring their

Lord Mayor Alderman Charles Bowman takes his sheep across London Bridge Lake Havasu Arizona

livestock across London Bridge to market at Smithfield (thus giving them a commercial advantage over non freemen). But the right then also extended to all animals going to market - cattle, geese, ducks, goats and sheep. However, as wool was the staple of English trade the idea of driving sheep seems to have been most resonant over the centuries. It still pertains today so that the Chamberlain's Court, where the freedom ceremony is performed, is well stocked with sheep and crooks and woolly tales.

The Woolmen realised that they were well placed to capitalise on this myth and promote their sheep. A pilot idea in 2013 has now been repeated annually and many people have now participated in the Annual Sheepdrive that it is a City tradition. Each year up to 600 people are given the privilege to exercise the so-called right of a freeman of the City of London to take their sheep over London Bridge. It is so popular that you have to book in advance (and pay) and the website goes live in April for the following September. You do not have to be a freeman to take part and everyone gets a certificate at the end to say that they have taken their sheep across London Bridge.

The sheep are driven across the bridge from north to south and on the first drive of the day there is usually a selection of important guest shepherds. In 2018 the Lord Mayor, Alderman Charles Bowman attended with the Lady Mayoress, Samantha, who is a Woolman and has her own flock. They were accompanied by Alan Titchmarsh who became a freeman during the year. When they come to the southern end of the bridge and the London Borough of Southwark they are met by the Guildable Manor of Southwark. The foreman of the Manor presents them with a jar of mint sauce. Prayers are also said in conjunction with Southwark Cathedral. The sheep are driven back towards the City and then spend the day enchanting the various volunteer shepherds who are booked to take their turn in driving the sheep back and forth over the Bridge.

The mastermind behind the scheme is Past Master Woolman, Bill Clark. Previously sheep have been taken across London Bridge by the World

The Guild of Young Freemen act as shepherds at the annual Woolmen's Sheep Drive (with the Sheriffs September 2018)

Traders in 2008 and a full bridge closure and extravaganza took place in 2009 on the 800th anniversary of the Bridge. But the Woolmen have now created an event in perpetuity that gives a wide variety of people great pleasure and enjoyment. Indeed they claim that this is the first sheepdrive as previous events have had sheep on leads, which is not so authentic. The British Red Cross have also had a sheep drive

with stuffed toy sheep on wheels as a fundraiser that produced some pretty odd looking sheep!

Recently Bill Clark was talking to the City Livery Club about setting up the event. Even he had not anticipated the effort and innovation that would be needed to create the event and keep it on the road.

Bill told the Club that he had to navigate a wide variety of regulations and bodies to get permission, a process that involved not only the City Corporation but also Transport for London and Defra as well as the RSPCA. The sheep are well cared for with a vet in attendance and rests and shade provided but there are still occasional protests at the

The Woolmen's Sheep Drive with Alan Titchmarsh

event. The sheep are provided by a farmer from Bedford who uses his sheep to train sheep dogs and they are often used for filming and TV. They are not just any old sheep!

People are encouraged to enter into the spirit of the day and many people dress up for the event. There is even a prize given for the best dressed. Bo Peep and Farmer Giles are regular figures as well

Sheep at the Sheep Drive

as numerous sheep and wolves in sheep's clothing. One year the animated Shaun the Sheep made an appearance as large replicas of Shaun were being placed all around London in order to raise funds for charity. While Alan Titchmarsh drove his sheep this year, in the past the drive has been started by Barbara Windsor, Nigel Mansell and Mary Berry. Such celebrities help publicise the event that gets coverage in the international press as well as national TV.

The Woolmen are helped by the Guild of Young Freeman and many volunteers on the day, not forgetting St John Ambulance. There is also a mix of other Livery Companies helping. The Worshipful Company of Information Technologists has revamped the website to allow online booking and to digitise a lot of the hard grind of forms and facts and figures. The Company of Public Relation Practitioners has stepped up to publicise and market the event. There is now sheep-related merchandise available to all. To date they have been blessed with good weather and a healthy financial return that goes partly to the Lord Mayor's Appeal and the Woolmen's Charitable Trust.

A sister event took place in 2018 while the Lord Mayor was visiting Lake Havasu, Arizona, where the old London Bridge has been erected in the desert. The Lord Mayor took part in a sheep drive across the old bridge - which from the photographs looked rather warm for the Lord Mayor and for the woolly sheep.

First published November 2018

When Dame Fiona Woolf was Lord Mayor she instituted the idea of City Giving Day (CGD). Over the past few years this has expanded and it is clearly stamped on the City's calendar as a day to celebrate. The idea of CGD is to encourage businesses to mark publicly the way that they contribute to society as responsible businesses and citizens. It is not just about raising money on the day; but to allow everyone to tell their story of volunteering, charity and philanthropy in the Square Mile and beyond. It also allows businesses to celebrate internally and externally the responsible business programmes that they undertake. It allows them to encourage their employees to volunteer or acts as a knowledge base to inform the wider business about what they do - in some cases businesses are so large that the efforts can be diffuse and unknown across their many departments. Some businesses use it as a day when they bring in charities that they work with to the offices or give their staff a volunteering day to do something different. What culminates in this day is the work of a year, of course.

All the Aldermen supporting the Lord Mayor at City Giving Day

The event is run by the Lord Mayor's Appeal, which aims to sign up businesses to celebrate the day. Each year the Lord Mayor encourages businesses to join in and this year a record number of over 300 businesses signed up. In the lead up there are many events, often at breakfast, to encourage the businesses as to how to use the day. Since the Plaisterers' charity is a significant donor to the Lord Mayor's Appeal we were invited to breakfast this year and our Learned Clerk ended up sitting next to the owner of the City AM newspaper and took a fetching photo pledging our commitment. Indeed, City AM is a major supporter and publishes vignettes in its daily newspaper spotlighting the various businesses in a free

Past Master Bill Mahony supporting the day 2018

The Plaisterers' Clerk Nigel Bamping supporting the City Giving Day breakfast at Mansion House

advertorial. The Plaisterers appeared on July 25th 2018.

City Giving Day 2018 (25th September) began at 8am when the Lord Mayor, many Aldermen and numerous City businesses came together in Guildhall Yard to start the celebrations. You might have guessed by the photo that the colour of the day is red and everyone is encouraged to wear this colour. It helps that the Aldermanic gowns are that colour too.

A very welcome addition this year was the Phoenix Past Masters' Association. Their year of 2015-16 coincided with the Shrievalty of the Lord Mayor Alderman Charles Bowman who is their Vice President. The Phoenix Masters have pledged to help the Lord Mayor in any way that they can during his year of office. This meant that our Phoenix Past Master, Bill Mahony, was present and very much involved.

After the early photo call the Lord Mayor, Sheriffs and Aldermen then toured around the City trying to visit as many of these businesses as possible to support and thank them for their work. Bill was paired with Alderman William Russell and he writes:

"I risked life and limb while being pedal power-driven around the City, which was a sea of red with Alderman William Russell on the CIBC World Markets' bus. We were joined by the Lord Mayor on a pedi-bus from Mansion House, before heading off to the Cheesegrater to meet Aon, who also were pedalling, but here Aon staff were riding in sequence for an endurance test. The Lord Mayor showed his genuinely impressive leg power on a static bike. Aon was raising money for its third year for Suited and Booted, a charity that prepares ex-service personnel for civilian work. The charity was cheering on.

"We visited offices where a crowd of enthusiastic brokers vied to build the highest mountain of Sugar Cubes (sugar traders). Next door The Great British Bake Off was being re-enacted, so we had energy to dash to St Paul's to watch The Tour de London on static bikes - very impressive!

"Then we joined Alderman Peter Estlin at The Bank of China who had staged a mad carnival-like exhibition on the 9th Floor of number 1 Lothbury with hundreds of staff manning stands to demonstrate the inclusion of all the countries on the Silk Road, and several random others. Each stall holder was trying to outshout his neighbours. The din was quite incredible - our memories have been scarred by one Chinese chap leaping around in a Pharaoh's outfit extolling the virtues of Egypt.

"In the afternoon I had one more call to make with

Alderman Alison Gowman visiting UBS in support of City Giving Day

Sheriff Tim Hailes, this time high-tailing it down to EY's splendid building in Canary Wharf. EY has been running a massive programme to encourage young people from underprivileged backgrounds to learn about the world of business and consider how a career in consultancy, or indeed any of EY's many clients might suit them. There we heard from one of the young people and she gave a very confident, articulate talk on how much she had learned."

My day as Alderman for Dowgate Ward was a little less frenetic but I called in on Nomura who were hosting a session with young students from local schools meeting Nomura staff to learn about working in the City; what they need to study and how to improve the chances of getting a job. I also called at UBS who had a morning of working with the charities that they had supported to get grants via the City Bridge Trust to learn about creating social investment opportunities.

All in all some 50 businesses were visited and the message of the importance of philanthropy and responsible business was clearly shouted from the very roof tops. The Lord Mayor said:

"There is really valuable work being done by City firms, benefiting society through business volunteering, fundraising events and philanthropic work. City Giving Day is a chance to shout out about this vital work, whilst at the same time encouraging others to get involved.

"It's clear to see that many firms are now making responsible business programmes and philanthropic activity a core part of their purpose, a rising trend which looks set to increase."

With grateful thanks to Past Master Bill Mahony.

First published May 2018

Some of you may have noticed the more than usually congested traffic and visible policing during the week of the Commonwealth Heads of Government Business Forum.

The City of London was very pleased to be asked by the Commonwealth Secretary-General (aka Alderman Baroness Patricia Scotland QC) to host the Business Forum meetings that accompany the main Heads of Government meeting. This was carried out in conjunction with the Commonwealth Enterprise and Investment Council. They monopolised the Guildhall and the Mansion House for three days from Monday April 16th to Wednesday 18th. Only the City could host such a series of high-profile meetings lunches and receptions with the highest security and without any mishaps.

The Prime Minister Mrs Theresa May opened the event in Guildhall. She spoke from the heart about the concerns of the Commonwealth. She said: "As we talked about their ideas and aspirations, about their vision for the future of the Commonwealth, I was struck by the vital role that businesses like yours have in tackling their concerns and giving substance to their ambitions. They called for cleaner oceans and greater sustainability. You can help deliver that by changing business practices and creating innovative new products and solutions. They called for action on youth unemployment. You, as entrepreneurs and business leaders, create the jobs and opportunities our young people need and, by driving our economies, you fund the schools and colleges that equip them with the skills they need."

Sir John Major with the Lord Mayor and Countess of Wessex on Tower Bridge

She went on to announce that the UK will be funding an all-new Commonwealth Standards Network that will support developing countries in particular to better meet existing international standards. She said she was also funding a Trade Facilitation Programme, to support and provide technical assistance to selected Commonwealth countries in implementing the World Trade Organisation's Trade Facilitation Agreement. But perhaps the most eye-catching announcement was the pledge to boost women's access to economic opportunity, and empower them to create and build their own businesses. This she has termed: SheTrades Commonwealth. This will offer Commonwealth-wide support to help countries break down gender barriers in international trade. She said: "It has been estimated that if women played the same role as men in labour markets, as much as $28 trillion could be added to global GDP by 2025."

The Lord Mayor and Chair of Policy and Resources (Catherine McGuinness) were very prominent in many of the sessions and led discussions in the business of trust, fintech, green finance, resilience and the digital economy. Many Government Ministers also took part; Liam Fox, Amber Rudd, and Matthew Hancock MP to name but three.

Lord Mayor at CHOGM

Two high-profile entertainments showcased the best of the City. On the Monday evening the Walkways of Tower Bridge were the setting for a party celebrating the work of the Queen Elizabeth Diamond Jubilee Trust (QEDJT). Its chair, former Prime Minister Sir John Major, greeted guests accompanied by your author (in her role as the Chair of the City Bridge Trust). We greeted such a variety of guests from Prime Ministers (Solomon Islands and Vanuatu), to MPs and from High Commissioners to the Lord Mayor. Our main guest was the Countess of Wessex. The QEDJT has been concentrating on eliminating avoidable blindness and especially tackling trachoma. Minister Penny Mordaunt MP, Secretary of State for International Development could not attend but sent a message pledging £20 million to aid the work. Sir John quipped that he was not so upset that a Minister could not attend at the last minute as long as they send along funds of £20 million to make up for their absence. To this was added the generosity of the world's leading ophthalmic

Alderman Baroness Scotland at CHOGM

lens manufacturer, Essilor, which pledged to expand its business and philanthropic programmes to meet the vision needs of 200 million people living with poor eyesight in the Commonwealth. Essilor will both improve the vision care infrastructure and provide 200 million people living below the poverty line with free ophthalmic lenses. It's safe to say the event was a remarkable success!

The other major ceremonial event was a dinner in the Guildhall entertaining 600 people from the Business Forum. The main guests were the Chancellor of the Exchequer and the President of South Africa. The Lord Mayor hosted the banquet with great aplomb and we were treated to the full delight of the Royal Household Trumpeters, the Pikemen and Musketeers and some uplifting music.

The President spoke movingly of the state of South Africa today - the legacy of Nelson Mandela who received the Honorary Freedom of the City of London in the very same Great Hall. The guest list was eclectic to say the least and many were intrigued to see Bill Gates on the top table - fresh from talks about reducing malaria across the Commonwealth.

The Forum ended with the Prince of Wales attending the conference and greeting many of the attendees.

The event demonstrates how the City can offer entertainment and create the right environment for people from all over the world to visit and find the right opportunities to network and do business. This is what the City does

Alderman Alison Gowman at CHOGM

best and it was greatly appreciated by the guests and by Government. It was an exhausting few days for all involved including the City Police, security and catering staff.

While this was a very high-profile event there are many such other events that the City regularly hosts in order to enhance the work of the City financial or the Government. Some criticise the City for this largesse and its use of the power and the influence that it exhibits. It seems that no one else could have fielded the breadth and depth of leaders in their field to speak at such events and to bring the world to its doorstep and open up the channels of communication and trade. Only the City of London can do this.

First published February 2016

In the 2013-14 Yearbook the Learned Clerk set out the history of The Honourable The Irish Society and the City Livery companies. This included the links with the Plaisterers who joined many of the other Livery companies in contributing to a syndicate to help with the infamous Ulster Plantations. This article will not repeat that very interesting information save to bring it to your mind that the Plantations were instituted in 1609 by James I. The Honourable the Irish Society (hereafter the Irish Society) was set up in 1613 to oversee the City of London estates in Northern Ireland. These estates constituted the rebuilding of Derry (renamed Londonderry), Coleraine and other parts of the Province. I want to start with what it is today and why I am a Member of the Court.

The Irish Society's assets are in part premises in Northern Ireland and an investment portfolio. The premises are the most interesting as they include the walls of the City of Derry (Londonderry),

Map of the Plantations in 1620

the fishing rights over the Rivers Foyle and Bann and the sporting rights over even larger tracts of Northern Ireland.

The Irish Society evolved from a land owning and management organisation of the 17th century into a self-funding, cross-community charitable organisation and continues to work today for the benefit of the community in County Londonderry, as laid down in the Royal Charters of 1613 and 1662, which govern its activities. The Irish Society is administered from offices in Coleraine, where the Secretary and Representative is based, and also in the City of London. It is led by a Governor, Deputy Governor and Court of Trustees. The Governor is always a Past Lord Mayor, currently Alderman Sir David Wootton and the Deputy Governor and Trustees are Aldermen and Common Council members. Having shown how closely linked it appears to the City, it is in fact a separate charity and is independently run and administered.

The Irish Society applies the income derived from its properties in Londonderry and Coleraine (including the fisheries and from its investment portfolio) to a wide range of local Northern Ireland

The Hon The Irish Society crest

causes. This is done under the guidance of a local Advisory Committee, composed of a cross-party selection of Councillors from Derry City & Coleraine (Strabane) District Council, who co-operate closely with the Society's local representative. The Mayor of Derry City is a member of the Committee, and the Chief Executive officers of all three Councils also attend meetings. The Society is careful not to cause any offence or difficulty in the community in its dealings and grant-making.

The grant-giving is driven by applications from individuals and local organisations - from amateur sports and senior citizens clubs, youth groups, community, residents, workers and health associations to schools and other educational bodies. In the past year about 110 grants averaging £400 were given out - some in conjunction with the Drapers and Clothworkers who recall their heritage in the Plantations.

The fishing rights have been quite a money-spinner but also a reason for investing in the local environment and habitat. Both local fishing clubs and international celebrities enjoy the fishing. Salmon fishing has always been the mainstay of the fisheries, but there are excellent trout waters and coarse fishing of an international standard too. In recent years the general crisis in salmon stocks has caused the

The 1613 Royal Charter creating the Society

sales to be reduced - not helped by unseasonal high river flows and increased summer rainfall. Needless to say the bailiffs are busy regulating the fishing, which has its fair share of poachers. When the Trustees visit it is always a delight to travel on the rivers and see the beautiful countryside in this part of the UK.

Indeed the Trustees do make traditionally three visits to Northern Ireland each year. In June the Governor attends a week of visits to school prize-givings and to other educational institutions. There are several schools founded by the Irish Society and many others to whom funding has been given over many years. Visits in March and October variously visit the properties, meet the local Mayors, Lord Lieutenants and other business people and the charities to whom grants are given. Over the years the Irish Society has been able to bridge divides in the community - not least by the Advisory Committee meetings.

In 2013 we marked the 400th anniversary of the grant of the Irish Society's Charter by King James I. It coincided with Derry (Londonderry) being the UK City of Culture and a large-scale cultural and business programme being built around the year. A rather irreverent opera called At Sixes and Sevens was written to be performed simultaneously in the Guildhalls of Londonderry and the City of London about the Plantations. A particularly galling title for the Skinners who lost considerable funds during the Plantations - due to the allocation to them of some of the worst land in Northern Ireland.

More importantly from a City business point of view, the Irish Society were instrumental in arranging an inward investment seminar in the City of London's Guildhall in 2013, in partnership with Invest Northern Ireland and focusing on cultural industries and sectors. That dynamic of linkage on a business front has continued and our Lord Mayor visited Belfast (not actually part of the Plantations) and Londonderry in December 2015.

During his trip the Lord Mayor attended a business meeting with Invest Northern Ireland, a dinner at the Titanic Centre, and a breakfast roundtable hosted by financial services firm Citi. He also met the Mayor of Derry-Londonderry and Martin McGuinness, Deputy First Minister of Northern Ireland.

Lord Mayor Mountevans said: "I am delighted that my first regional visit [was] ... to Belfast. It's a strategically important centre for the UK in which the financial and professional services community plays a key role, supporting over 31,000 jobs and providing £2bn (7.4%) of regional GVA and 4.5% of regional employment. My visit will help build the ties that can generate growth in both our regions. Success for Belfast is success for London too."

The visit was testament to the work of the Irish Society and its close links with the City of London and the County Londonderry community - working for the best of ties and engagement between us.

The Governor of The Honourable the Irish Society is now Alderman Sir Andrew Parmley and the local government areas in Northern Ireland have been reorganised and renamed.

First published January 2016

The Clerk was somewhat perturbed to find a large Police operation outside Plaisterers' Hall a few weeks ago - luckily I was on hand to allay his worries of any major incident and explained the City of London Police's Project Servator: the name given to unpredictable, highly visible police deployments, designed to deter, detect and disrupt a wide range of criminal activity.

City Police logo

Even though I serve on the City of London Police Committee, I was not breaching any confidential information because the Police are keen to inform the public about the ground-breaking and intelligence-led measures they are taking. Indeed, there was a news item on Radio 4's News at One in December and regular pieces have appeared in CityAM and the Standard.

The City Police has always sought to be prepared for every eventuality. When, in 1992, the IRA bomb exploded in the City, the City of London Corporation and the City of London Police introduced the Ring of Steel. This was initially a series of barriers that looked like large red and white lego bricks; but its purpose was to reduce the access points into the City and at each such entrance to have a manned Police presence and/or CCTV. This has proved resilient and coupled with ANPR (automatic number plate readers) means that any vehicle coming into the City is effectively vetted within seconds of triggering the ANPR system. However, times change and the City Police have realised the need to upgrade and improve this in order to meet new criminal and terrorist threats.

Project Servator at Bank of England

Operation or Project Servator is a new specific way of policing that has been pioneered by the City of London Police to protect our City. Under Project Servator the Police will flood a particular area of the City on a random (to the criminals) basis saturating it with both Police Officers in

Project Servator on Tower Bridge

Project Servator using mounted police

uniform, on horseback, motorcycle, with dogs but also with undercover officers. They will be placed over the length of a road or area effectively giving the police a good period of time collectively to view the behavioural pattern of vehicles and pedestrians. The Officers are trained to spot people carrying out terrorist reconnaissance or otherwise taking evasive action (when they view uniformed police in the vicinity). Thus collectively they are jointly deployed to boost efforts to thwart any atrocity on British soil as well as being an obvious deterrent to any criminal action. You will be able to envisage that the length of London Wall with the pull-in at the end of Noble Street is an ideal location for spotting and stopping vehicles without too much disruption to the traffic flow.

Officers are specially trained in behavioural detection. They are not just aiming at anyone 'looking shifty' but are basing their views on evidence apparent from behavioural training, as was reported on Radio 4.

During the pilot of the scheme detecting suspicious behaviours it was clear that it had deterred hostile reconnaissance, which is a precursor to terrorist planning for a potential attack and involves the collection of information so terrorists can maximise the effectiveness of their violent actions. It was later claimed that 'chatter' among jihadis was understood to have referred to the police operation and confirmed it had been a deterrent.

The City Police website states: The project involves new tactics and cutting-edge training for police officers that will help deter those from carrying out hostile reconnaissance and help detect those with malicious intent. It also increases the opportunity for interaction between police officers and the public, provides further reassurance to the public and helps deter and detect other criminal perpetrators. These new tactics will mean a more enhanced and strategic approach to protecting the Square Mile and is part of the force's drive to deploy its resources more effectively.

The tactics provide reassurance to the general public while deterring would-be criminals and making a wide range of criminals (from petty criminals, to extreme protest through to terrorists) easier to detect by specially trained officers. This use of specially trained officers has been proven to be very effective in detecting criminals and those with criminal intent. Along with supporting information and materials, people will see more high-profile deployments in and around communities and at key locations. These deployments will vary from one day to the next.

The Police are keen that if you see any suspicious activity you should report it by calling 101. Use 999 if an immediate response is required.

As well as being vigilant and reporting anything suspicious, a pivotal part of Project Servator is telling people about what's happening. It is really important that the public understand the nature of the operations and, crucially, feel reassured rather than alarmed. That's why I was happy to reassure Nigel and to ensure that the Plaisterers are well informed and playing their part in policing the City.

First published May 2019

You will have heard of the Square Mile of the City of London. The City of London Corporation, together with the Barbican Centre, Guildhall School of Music and Drama, London Symphony Orchestra and Museum of London have developed that idea and formed a partnership called the Culture Mile - a major destination for culture and creativity in the City of London.

It is an ambitious and transformational initiative that shows the benefits that can be achieved from the creation of a vibrant cultural area in the north-west corner of the City which will develop over the next 10 to 15 years. It stretches just under a mile from Farringdon to Moorgate. It will have at its heart creative exchange, cultural collaboration and learning.

The core participants are all internationally acclaimed organisations in their own right and some partnerships already operate across these institutions, but working further together and led by the City

Celebrating 150 years of Smithfield Market August 2018

of London Corporation, they will transform the area, improving their offer to audiences with imaginative collaborations, outdoor programming and events seven days a week. Links between venues will be improved and major enhancements to the streets and wider public realm will enliven the area which, as Culture Mile expands and flourishes, will be regenerated.

This co-operation and enhancement of the area is already under way to the benefit of all. For example, the newest exhibition at the Museum of London, called Beasts of London, is a work co-created with the Guildhall School using their skills to create a fully immersive digital installation using video projection mapping. In August last year the Museum led the celebration of 150 years of the current Smithfield Market with a recreation of the medieval St Bartholomew's Fair that was a riot (literally) of fun in the past. It proved very popular in 2018 as well with events for all the family to enjoy. Beech Street was closed to traffic one weekend in May 2018 to create a light installation that was immersive and overwhelming in scale. There is still a kinetic tapestry on the walls of Beech Street by artist Jason Bruges. The work translates imagery, video, sound and binary data into tangible marks. You have to see it to understand the full artistic and cultural meaning. All of this is testing out how streets can have alternative uses and making Beech Street a better place and route through the spine of the Culture Mile.

The opening of Crossrail's new Elizabeth Line brings connections at Farringdon and Moorgate, which will make it much easier to travel to and from the City. Around 1.5 million additional visitors a year will be within a 45-minute journey of the area when the Elizabeth Line becomes fully operational. Farringdon will have direct access to three major London airports with a 30-minute journey time to London Heathrow. It will be the only place where London Underground, Thameslink and Crossrail all interlink and will be one of the busiest stations in the UK, making the area more connected than ever to London and beyond.

There are three major building projects associated with Culture Mile that enhance its potential scale and ambition: the new Museum of London at West Smithfield, due to open in 2024; the proposed Centre for Music, for which the preferred site is currently occupied by the Museum of London and the transformation of Beech Street, which will become a crucial axis for the Culture Mile. The City of London Corporation is assessing how best to transform Beech Street to make it a more welcoming environment, particularly for pedestrians and cyclists, including new measures to improve air quality, introduce retail units and providing better access to the existing cultural destinations either side of it.

Colourful road crossing towards Beech Street

The City of London Corporation is working to improve the environment and urban realm across Culture Mile through a programme that delivers better way-finding, signage, green spaces, lighting, public information and art installations. This strategy forms part of a City-wide programme of public realm improvements across the Square Mile including improving air quality through a new Low Emission Neighbourhood around the Barbican and Golden Lane Estate area. This strategy will aim to improve the look and feel of the area so as to attract more people and make it a nicer and healthier environment for the residents, businesses and visitors.

Catherine McGuinness, Policy Chair at the City of London Corporation said: "We are redefining the City of London, so that the Square Mile becomes known and admired as much for being a world-class cultural destination, as for its position as a leading global financial centre. Culture has been at its heart for centuries, alongside commerce, and now more than ever, arts and culture are vital to the UK economy and our position in the world. As one of the country's largest funders of cultural activities, we stand firmly behind Culture Mile. There is no doubt that Culture Mile will transform the area and in the face of Brexit send a signal to the world that London is - and will always be - a welcoming, open, and resolutely internationalist city."

Sharon Ament, Director, Museum of London; Sir Nicholas Kenyon, Managing Director, Barbican Centre; Kathryn McDowell, Managing Director, London Symphony Orchestra; Lynne Williams, Principal Guildhall School, agreed a statement that said: "This is a once-in-a-generation opportunity to regenerate the north-west of the City from Farringdon to Moorgate and to work together to transform Culture Mile into a world-leading cultural and creative destination. With the arrival of Crossrail, vastly increased numbers of people will have access to the area; Culture Mile is at the start of its journey and the partners will collaborate more closely, improve the environment, provide better access, enliven the area with outdoor programming, be more family friendly and celebrate learning at its core. We will develop a wider network of organisations who share a commitment to help transform the area over the next decade and to create a vibrant creative community."

The Culture Mile is in the north-west corner of the City of London and covers 45 hectares/110 acres, which is over 15% of the total area of the Square Mile. It has a blend of ancient and modern with Roman walls, medieval churches and livery halls close to new Crossrail stations, modern apartment blocks and a steady pipeline of cutting edge office

Proposals for new Centre For Music

developments and this is what makes Culture Mile unique. There is also a growing community of city workers, residents, students, cultural and creative industry workers and visitors. However, there are other nearby venues that are linked in to the whole scheme - The Charterhouse, LSO St Luke's and Clerkenwell's own deep history such as St John's Gate and Museum. Thus the links are also being made with neighbouring Islington in order to expand the reach of this initiative and draw in the whole of London to the Culture Mile.

Beech Street Barbican light show - Tunnel Visions: Array

APPENDIX: JARGON BUSTING

First published September/October 2015

The Corporation of London exercises the role of the City's local authority, based at Guildhall. While it is in part run in the same way as any other local authority, it does have its idiosyncrasies … a description as set out below has many assumed words and ideas that this list of useful words and definitions may help you understand better.

The non-party political Common Council consists of 25 Aldermen and 100 members (25 of whom are Deputies) led by the Chief Commoner, all of whom receive no pay or allowances, elected by the voters (including business voters) of their ward, and appointed at Wardmotes (presided over by the ward's Alderman, who is attended by his or her mace-bearing Beadle), supported by paid staff and officers. Council meetings are chaired by the Lord Mayor (who is an Alderman, but who has been elected to the office of Lord Mayor by the City's Liverymen, at a meeting of Common Hall, and taken office at a Silent Ceremony), who is supported through his/her year in office by, inter alios, two Sheriffs (also elected by the Liverymen, at a separate Common Hall) and a permanent team of Esquires, who have both administrative and ceremonial roles. The 'normal' work of a local authority is carried out by staff headed by the Town Clerk (the CEO) and including a Remembrancer (who also has a ceremonial role) and a Comptroller and City Solicitor.

ALDERMAN
The City has one Alderman for each of its 25 wards. They are elected every six years by the voters in their ward (and may stand for re-election at any time within that six-year period), and must retire from office on reaching the age of 70. To stand for office a person must be aged at least 21, a British subject, a Freeman of the City and satisfy the requirements of office of a Police and Crime Commissioner or be a JP. They are unpaid, and receive no allowances. One of the Aldermen is elected annually by Liverymen, at Common Hall, to become Lord Mayor. An Alderman is effectively a member of the Council who has aspirations to become Lord Mayor, and consequently has a heavier workload - performing all the duties of a Common Councilman as well as those restricted to Aldermen.

BEADLE
There are currently 29 Ward Beadles in the 25 wards (the three largest wards have two or three Beadles), who are elected at the annual Wardmote. Their role is largely ceremonial, and they accompany their Alderman at formal City occasions (such as Common Hall), dressed in their robes and tricorn hats, and carrying a Ward Mace.

CHAMBERLAIN OF LONDON
A high officer of the Corporation, appointed by the Court of Common Council; effectively, the City's Chief Financial Officer.

CHIEF COMMONER
The Chief Commoner is elected annually by the Court of Common Council, for a one-year term, and takes office on the first Council meeting following the annual Wardmotes. He or she is the foremost representative of the Commoners.

CITY MARSHAL
One of the Lord Mayor's Esquires, who leads formal processions (on horseback at the Lord Mayor's Show).

CITY SURVEYOR

A high officer of the Corporation, appointed by the Court of Common Council, who, among other things runs the City's large property portfolio.

COMMON COUNCILMAN, or COMMON COUNCILLOR

There are 100 Common Councilmen (Councillors in any other Local Authority) elected by the voters of their wards every four years, in March, at a Wardmote. Each Ward, depending on the number of voters, has between two and 10 Common Councilmen, who must be a British subject (or EU citizen) aged at least 18, a Freemen of the City and a Voter in the City (not necessarily in the Ward in which they stand). Like the Aldermen, they are unpaid, receive no allowances, and are virtually all independent members. (The City does not currently have a party political system although five members were elected in 2017 under the Labour Party banner). They act in the same way as Councillors elsewhere - chairing and attending meetings to ensure the smooth running of the City. Each member is allocated a number of ward committees (committees which have representatives of each ward, such as the Finance and Planning and Transportation Committees) by their Deputy, and can stand for election to many more (such as Police and Barbican Centre Committees).

COMMONER

A member of the Court of Common Council who is not an Alderman.

COMMON CRYER AND SERJEANT AT ARMS

One of the Lord Mayor's Esquires, this officer is also known as the Macebearer, who carries the Mace on ceremonial occasions, and calls for order at the start of Meetings of Common Council and Common Hall.

COMMON HALL

There are two Common Halls each year, held at Guildhall; these are meetings of Liverymen to elect the Lord Mayor and the Sheriffs. One is on Midsummer Day (June 24th), or the Monday following if Midsummer Day falls on a weekend, to elect the Sheriffs, some largely ceremonial posts (Ale Conners and Bridgemasters), the Auditors and the Livery Committee. The other is held on Michaelmas Day (September 29th), or the Monday following if Michaelmas day falls on a weekend, to elect the Lord Mayor. All Liverymen, who have been Liverymen since May of the previous year may attend, and they, and only they, are the voters. The Shrieval election is sometimes contested, and if there are two clear winners they are elected; if the result is in dispute, and a poll is called for, this is held at a subsequent Common Hall two weeks later, although candidates are urged to accept the findings of Common Hall and not to demand a poll.

COMPTROLLER AND CITY SOLICITOR

A high officer of the Corporation, appointed by the Court of Common Council, who is the City's senior legal officer.

COURT OF ALDERMEN

The 25 Aldermen, in addition to being part of the Court of Common Council, meet separately from time to time in the Aldermen's Court on the West side of Guildhall Yard. Among other things, they agree the Freedom of the City for those who apply through a Livery Company and regulate and approve new Livery Companies.

COURT OF COMMON COUNCIL

The Court of Common Council (CoCo) is the formal meeting (in other local authorities it would be a council meeting) of the 100 Common Councilmen and the 25 Aldermen. Meetings are held 9 times a year, at 1pm on a Thursday, and are presided over by the Lord Mayor, run by the Town Clerk, and attended by the senior officers of the City of London (Chamberlain, Surveyor, etc.). CoCo meetings are open to the public, although the public will be excluded for any matters of a 'non-public' nature (normally at the end of the meeting)

DEPUTY

One of the Common Councilmen in each Ward is appointed Ward Deputy by the Alderman at the annual Wardmote. The Deputy's duties are to support the Alderman and to act as team leader to the Ward's Common Councilmen.

ELECTIONS

There are City-wide elections for Common Councilmen every four years, in March, when all 100 seats may be contested (the next elections are in March 2021). The 25 Aldermen are each elected for a six-year term, but are not all elected at the same time, and may put themselves up for re-election at any time during their six years, so Aldermanic elections are held sporadically. A by-election will be triggered by the death or retirement of an Alderman, or when an Alderman reaches the age of 70. The elections of the Lord Mayor and the Sheriffs are held at Common Hall.

ESQUIRES

The Esquires, based at Mansion House, are the paid officers of the Lord Mayor's household who also have ceremonial roles (City Marshal, Swordbearer and Common Cryer). One of them will normally accompany the Lord Mayor to every function. When acting outside of their ceremonial roles they are termed programme managers and there is a senior programme manager based in Mansion House who is not an Esquire. In addition, the senior Mansion House official is the Private Secretary and Chief of Staff to the Lord Mayor who runs the House and is responsible for all matters under the Lord Mayor. In 2017, the Private Secretary took responsibility for the Central Criminal Court (The Old Bailey) as well and his new job title is Executive Director of Mansion House and Central Criminal Court.

FREEDOM OF THE CITY

Apart from the Honorary Freedom of the City, the highest honour the City can bestow and which is given to very few people, there are three ways of obtaining the Freedom of the City. (1) By redemption (ie payment), either by personal application or via a Livery Company; (2) By Patrimony (and thence by right), which can only be given if one parent was a Freeman before the birth of the applicant: and (3) by Servitude, the route for an apprentice who has served a full apprenticeship to a Freeman. Despite popular myths, the Freedom confers no rights and privileges whatsoever.

FREEMAN

A Freeman of the City is a person who has the Freedom of the City; a Freeman of a Livery Company may, or may not be, a Freeman of the City, but will need to apply for the City Freedom in order to become a Liveryman. Freemen cannot attend Common Hall.

GOWNS

On ceremonial occasions, Aldermen wear scarlet gowns (they wear violet gowns at the meeting of Common Hall, Wardmotes and the Silent Ceremony). Common Councilmen wear blue gowns (the colour is Mazarine blue, and the gown is sometimes referred to as a Mazarine gown).

LIVERYMAN
A Liveryman is a full member of one of the Livery Companies, is eligible to vote at Common Hall, and is therefore one of those who elects the Sheriffs and is part of the election of the Lord Mayor.

LORD MAYOR
To become Lord Mayor, a person must be an Alderman, and have previously served as one of the two Sheriffs. He/she is first nominated by the Court of Aldermen and then nominated on Michaelmas Day, by Liverymen at Common Hall (but actually elected following such endorsement on the same day by the Aldermen who withdraw from Common Hall to have a secret ballot). The Lord Mayor takes office at the Silent Ceremony on the Friday before the Lord Mayor's Show. The Lord Mayor lives at Mansion House for the Mayoral year, presides over meetings of the Court of Aldermen and of Common Council, and spends the year promoting the City in this country and abroad. The post is unpaid. The Lord Mayor's Banquet, held on the Monday after the Lord Mayor's Show, is a dinner held by the incoming Lord Mayor in honour of the outgoing one.

LORD MAYOR LOCUM TENENS
When the Lord Mayor is unable to attend an event (for example, a meeting of Common Council, or a formal lunch or dinner) he/she will normally appoint an Alderman who has already served in the office of Lord Mayor, to represent him/her as "Lord Mayor Locum Tenens".

LORD MAYOR'S SHOW
The Lord Mayor's Show is held on the second Saturday in November, and is when the Lord Mayor processes to the Royal Courts of Justice to swear allegiance to the Sovereign (and, on the way, receives a blessing from the Dean at St Paul's)

MACEBEARER
See Common Cryer and Serjeant at Arms

RECORDER OF LONDON
The Recorder is the Senior Judge at the Old Bailey, and is responsible for running the election of the Lord Mayor at the Michaelmas Common Hall. The Common Serjeant is the second senior Judge who also plays a role at Common Hall.

REMEMBRANCER
A high officer of the Corporation, appointed by the Court of Common Council; effectively, the City's Chief of Protocol.

SHERIFFS
Two Sheriffs are elected each year, at the Midsummer Day Common Hall; in most years one is an Alderman (who becomes the Aldermanic Sheriff), and one is not (the non-Aldermanic Sheriff, who used to be referred to as the Lay Sheriff), but in some years the Court of Aldermen consider that the number of Aldermen eligible to become Lord Mayor is too small, and they will put forward two Aldermanic candidates; in such a case, it is the convention that there will be no non-Aldermanic candidate. Anyone standing for Sheriff must be nominated by 15 Liverymen, and, for the non-Aldermanic post, the only qualification is that he or she must be a Freeman of the City (although it is the norm that candidates are Liverymen).
The Sheriffs take office on September 28th (or the nearest working day if the 28th is a weekend) and celebrate this at the Sheriffs' Breakfast (a lengthy luncheon); their duties are, inter alia, to attend and

support the Lord Mayor (one or other of the Sheriffs will normally accompany the Lord Mayor on any formal function), and to entertain Her Majesty's Judges to luncheon each day at the Central Criminal Court (the Old Bailey), which is where they have accommodation for their year.

SILENT CEREMONY
The Lord Mayor is admitted, and takes over from his/her predecessor, at the Silent Ceremony (so called because it is conducted in silence, in the Great Hall of Guildhall) on the Friday before the Lord Mayor's Show.

SWORDBEARER
One of the Lord Mayor's Esquires, whose ceremonial duties include carrying the City sword on formal occasions. The Swordbearer wears the 'cap of maintenance' - the fur cap is depicted as the crest on the City coat of arms.

TOWN CLERK
The City of London's paid Chief Executive, appointed by the Court of Common Council.

VOTERS
All residents have a vote. Uniquely, the City also has a Business Vote whereby - depending on the number of staff they employ in the City - a business may have a certain number of voters (who may be nominated in any way the firm wishes, and who will be City workers). Sole traders and equity partners in businesses may also register to vote in the same way as existed throughout England and Wales until the 1960s.

WARD
A ward is an electoral division, and the City is divided into 25, each of which is represented by one Alderman and from two to 10 Common Councilmen depending on its number of voters. Most wards have a Ward Club, which is a mainly social organisation based on the ward.

WARDMOTE
Every ward has an annual Wardmote in March; this is an occasion when voters in the ward can question their local members, and when the Alderman will appoint the Ward Deputy and Beadle. Every fourth year (the next being in 2021) the ward elections coincide with the Wardmote, and in those years the names of those standing for Common Council are read out by the Alderman, and the candidates have the opportunity of addressing the voters present (and the voters to question the candidates) and (in the case of an uncontested election, the candidates are declared members for the next four years). If there are more candidates than there are places, the Wardmote will be adjourned until after the election (which usually takes place on the next day), and at the adjourned Wardmote the results of the ballot will be announced and the successful candidates will swear an oath of office. A Wardmote is also held whenever a casual vacancy occurs in a ward (i.e. a by-election) in the same way as a scheduled Wardmote.

© Museum of London

Proceeds from the sale of this book will be donated to the Museum of London.

The Museum tells the story of the capital from 450,000BC to modern times, with the Museum of London located on London Wall, near St. Paul's and the Museum of London Docklands located near Canary Wharf. It is an award winning organisation that sits at the heart of London's past, present and future and is a key member of the City's Culture Mile.

The Museum of London's galleries vividly tell the story of the city and its people, highlighting iconic moments in London's history such as the arrival of the Romans, the Great Fire of London and the London 2012 Olympic Games. The Museum of London Docklands is located in a 200-year-old warehouse situated close to the River Thames at the heart of Canary Wharf with the unique Port and River Archive situated within the building. The Museum receives over a million visitors across both sites each year including over 150,000 schoolchildren. The Archaeological Archive based at Mortimer Wheeler House in Shoreditch, Hackney, is the largest archaeological archive in Europe and cares for more than six million objects across the collections.

© Museum of London

The Museum allows people to discover the fascinating history of our capital city, from prehistory to today, inspiring a passion for London. Looking forward, plans are underway to create a new Museum of London amongst the beautiful market buildings of West Smithfield, creating a new home for

© Museum of London

the story of London.

The Plaisterers are delighted to support the Museum in their work with schools and, in particular, the Special Educational Needs and Disabilities Programme. This sector-leading programme offers free, tailored workshops to schools, making London's history accessible to children facing a wide range of challenges, ensuring that no one is excluded. The team work with around 1,600 young people each year, providing workshops both at school and

© Museum of London

at the Museum, making each one bespoke and thoroughly adapted to the needs of the group.

Your support in buying this book will help the Museum to provide this invaluable service, which teachers describe as "fantastic".